CIRCLING THE SUN

CIRCLING THE SUN

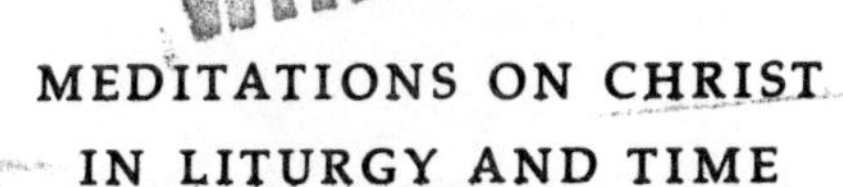

MEDITATIONS ON CHRIST IN LITURGY AND TIME

ROBERT D. PELTON

WITH INTRODUCTION BY VIRGIL C. FUNK

THE PASTORAL PRESS
WASHINGTON, D.C.

For Margaret, my mother;
Mark, my father;
Bill, my stepfather;

and

for Catherine, my spiritual mother;
Fr. Cal, my spiritual father;
Fr. Eddie, my friend.

Grateful acknowledgment is made to the following publisher for permission to quote from its published works:

From "Little Gidding" in *Four Quartets* by T.S. Eliot, copyright © 1936 by Harcourt Brace Jovanovich, Inc.; copyright © 1963, 1964, by T.S. Eliot. Reprinted by permission of the publisher.

ISBN 0-912405-14-7

The Pastoral Press
225 Sheridan Street, NW
Washington, D.C. 20011
(202) 723-5800

The Pastoral Press is the publications division of the National Association of Pastoral Musicians, a membership organization of musicians and clergy dedicated to fostering the art of musical liturgy.

Printed in the United States of America

Cover illustration adapted from a 15th-century Armenian bishop's stole by Donna J. Suprenant of Madonna House

Cover and text design by Paul Gunzelmann

CONTENTS

FEASTS AND SEASONS

1 THE BIRTH OF LIGHT

2 THE COMING OF FIRE

ORDINARY TIME

3 | THE MASTER OF LIFE

4 | THINGS AS THEY ARE

INTRODUCTION

To introduce these meditations on the way Christ comes to meet us in liturgy and time is to introduce the reader not only to the material, but to the author's context in writing this book. First the material.

The earth's circling the sun: in itself this is an image of time and its passage. Through the incarnation it has become a vivid icon of Christ's presence in his people—and in all creation. God not only entered time; he transformed it, making it a vessel of the holy action of his love. We embrace this new sacramental time as we travel through it yearly. The liturgical year, which this book beholds, reflects on, and celebrates, is more than an arbitrary reading of the secular calendar to suit the Church's theological and catechetical aims. The Church year is God's idea, not ours. God gave the Jews a liturgical calendar, and his Son lived it until the moment of Calvary, when he breathed forth his Spirit in it to make it something new. Christ chose to die and rise after the new moon of Passover and to mark his own passing over into glory with a new covenant meal in his own blood. Moreover, he ascended to the Father after forty days and bestowed the first-fruits of the Spirit on the Church ten days later, on the Jewish feast of Pentecost. Thus he gave to the new time of the new age a specific shape that the Church came to understand and embody in its historical development.

This book sees our passage through the riches of the new time as a journey into God's love for us in Christ. In the first part, "Feasts and Seasons," it focuses on the beginnings of the liturgical year during Advent-Christmas-Epiphany ("The Birth of Light") and on its climax in Lent-Easter-Pentecost ("The Coming of Fire"). The second part, "Ordinary Time," is also divided into two sections. The first, "The Master of Life," looks at Christ as the Lord-always-with-us and listens to him as he shows us the meaning of the Gospel life he has given us. The second section, "Things as They Are," moves into the depths of ordinary time. As in autumn, it deals with memory and reflection, the discovery of the limitless Kingdom present just where the fading sun discloses the fact of human limits. It ends where the book began, waiting for the One who waits for us. And if we have remembered well, we will know that he has met us and waits with us.

But in an unusual way, Robert Pelton has written these meditations about his own personal journey through time, and marvelously, about our own journeys. For Robert Pelton is a convert, a member of Madonna House Apostolate, a priest, a poustinik, and most recently, the director of priests of Madonna House.

Born and raised in Cleveland, Ohio, Bob came from a family with deep Protestant roots and a keen awareness of his exceptional intellectual ability and personal charm. At 20, while majoring in English at Yale University, he was jolted in his intellectual pursuit of truth and his search for faith by a friend from high school, Gail, and her best friend at Oberlin College, Marilyn. After spending time at Madonna House, they had set aside their own plans – a year of study in England for Gail, a cherished music scholarship for Marilyn – to follow the call of Christ: Marilyn to Madonna House and celibacy and Gail to Grailville to prepare for Christian marriage. Where was God? How to find Jesus Christ? He seemed, to Bob as well as to his friends, to be working powerfully at Madonna House. Within the year, Bob Pelton had put aside his established life, entered the Catholic Church with Catherine Doherty as his godmother, joined Madonna House, and made plans to enter the seminary.

Bob was ordained to the priesthood in 1963 for full time service in the Madonna House Apostolate, which has its training center in Combermere, Ontario. Madonna House is a community of laymen, laywomen and priests. It was founded by Catherine de Hueck Doherty on this simple mandate from the Lord:

> Arise – go! Sell all you possess...give it directly, personally to the poor. Take up My cross (their cross) and follow Me – going to the poor – being poor – being one with them – one with Me.
>
> Little – be always little...simple – poor – childlike,
>
> Preach the Gospel WITH YOUR LIFE – WITHOUT COMPROMISE – listen to the Spirit – He will lead you.
>
> Do little things exceedingly well for love of Me.
>
> Love – love – love, never counting the cost.

Go into the market place and stay with Me... pray... fast... pray always... fast.

Be hidden – be a light to your neighbor's feet. Go without fears into the depth of men's hearts... I shall be with you.

Pray always. I WILL BE YOUR REST.

To find his way to live this intense spiritual life, Fr. Bob was sent by Madonna House for many years of graduate study. He was eventually led to the University of Chicago Divinity School, where he studied history of religions under Mircea Eliade and other notable scholars. But that was not his path. When he finished his doctorate, he returned to Madonna House in Combermere, where a synthesis of the intellectual world and the world of the heart took place in the context of poustinia. This book embodies that synthesis.

Poustinia is a Russian word meaning "desert" – a place apart, in the country a secluded cabin, in the city a bare room containing only a bed, a table, a chair, an icon, a large cross, and a Bible. But poustinia also means the silence and solitude one seeks, not for their own sake, but in order to be still and listen to the Word of God. Here are the simple directives of Catherine Doherty to those entering the poustinia:

> For those of you who go into the poustinia for a day or two, this is the essence of it: to fold the wings of your intellect. In this civilization of the West everything is sifted through your heads.... The poustinia brings you into contact first and foremost with solitude. Secondly, it brings you in contact with God. Even if you don't feel anything at all, the fact remains that you have come to have a date with God, a very special rendezvous. You have said to the Lord, "Lord, I want to take this 24 hours out of my busy life and I want to come to you because I am very tired. The world is not the way you want it, and neither am I. I want to come and rest on your breast as St. John the Beloved. That's why I have come to this place."...
>
> St. Paul says, "Pray without ceasing" (1 Thes 5:17). Prayer is the source and the most intimate part of our lives. "When you pray, go into your room, close the door and pray to your Father in secret" (Mt 6:6). These words of Our Lord mean that you must enter into yourself and make a sanctuary there; the secret place is the human heart. The life of prayer – its intensity, its depth, its rhythm – is the measure of our spiritual health and reveals us to ourselves.... [When the poustinik] knows how to be silent, true prayer is found. Here he is mysteriously visited.[1]

---

[1]Catherine de Hueck Doherty, *Poustinia: Christian Spirituality of the East for Western Man* (Notre Dame, IN: Ave Maria Press, 1975), pp. 73-74.

And here are Fr. Pelton's words of reflection on this experience:

> The deepest purpose of this way of prayer is that it become an inner way of life. You go out to the desert so that the Lord you meet there can lead you to the hidden place of your own Spirit. You enter silence and solitude so that he may fill you with silence and make your solitude a place of welcome for whoever comes to you. You go out to listen to the Lord so that you can learn to hear him knocking at the door of your heart every day, so that you can hear his quiet voice, and open to him, and let him feed you, every day, with the infinite depths of his life, which he is already sharing with you in the Holy Spirit. You open yourself to his word so that you can speak it to all you meet—perhaps in speech, more probably in humble love and service, always in union with him who has chosen to make you and all his Father's children his best-loved dwelling on earth.

All Christians are, in fact, called to intense intimacy with the Lord. At Madonna House some feel called to the poustinia one day every week or every month. Others "become" poustiniks. The latter spend part of each week alone in a poustinia, part with the rest of the community. While in solitude, their life is simple. They pray and fast, but unlike those who spend one day in poustinia, the poustinik also keeps a garden, chops firewood, studies and writes a bit, and receives as Christ whomever he sends to visit. From January 13, 1975 until April 10, 1984, when he was elected director of the Madonna House priests, Bob Pelton lived three days a week in poustinia and the other four with the rest of the Madonna House community. These meditations were written during those years.

No introduction to Bob Pelton would be complete without an introduction to Catherine Doherty, Fr. John Callahan, and Fr. Eddie Doherty. Fr. Callahan was Bob's spiritual father. He baptized him, directed him, guided him in the priesthood, sent him to graduate school, gave him permission to enter the poustinia, and finally, with his death, called Bob to serve Madonna House in a new way. Eddie Doherty, the well-known crime reporter of the '20s and '30s, married Catherine in 1943. He founded Madonna House with her in May, 1947, and edited the Madonna House monthly newspaper, "Restoration," until his death in 1975. In 1969, at the age of 78, Eddie was ordained priest in the Melkite Rite. The reader will undoubtedly touch something of Fr. Eddie's delight in everything God showed him through these meditations written by one of his many spiritual children.

Catherine Doherty cannot really be introduced. Those who know her, love her. An introduction to Bob Pelton is an introduction to Catherine Doherty. And an introduction to Catherine Doherty is an introduction to Jesus. "The world," she writes, "rejects God because it only knows *about* him." "But," she continues,

> if the world knew him through his own revelation of himself to us in the poustinia of our hearts, then it could not reject him. . . . Then love would enter the world through us. We could speak his word to the world if we lived in the poustinia of our hearts.[2]

It is the deepest hope of the National Association of Pastoral Musicians in presenting this meditative book on the seasons of the Church's liturgical year, that each reader will discover the beauty of the Lord who is with us always.

Virgil C. Funk

---

[2]*Poustinia*, p. 214.

CIRCLING THE SUN

FEASTS AND SEASONS

1 THE BIRTH OF LIGHT

CONTEMPLATING

Contemplate me:
Draw me into the center of your eye,
Imprint me on your retinal wall,
Plunge me into the gray well of your cortex,
Fix me in your concepts,
Let your blood carry my name
Into your heart.

My beloved,
Let us do simple things together:
Speak of seasons and friends that live
Again and meet in our words;
Swim and feel the water slide between
And join our skins;
Let the sun mute our flesh and voices
As we knead the earth with careful hands.
Above all, let us eat,
Stuff ourselves with pasta and salad
Or dream of Corfu with feta and olives,
Let ripe tomatoes and buttered corn drip
Down our laughing chins and
Even let us feast in a labyrinth
Of coquilles, roast duck, and baked Alaska.
Let us, above all, remember
With bread and wine.

O contemplate me, my beloved,
In bread and wine.
O my Christ, fill me with your gaze
From the exact center of the bread
From the very depth of the cup.
Let your blood carry my name

Into your heart and out
Into your lungs, your mouth:
Breathe me into the clover-scented air
When you speak the morning into life.
Slip me like oil into the rivers and
Set me burning in the sky
To bless the slowly growing earth.
O my Christ,
Make me your food.

FINDING TIME

Where does it go, anyway—time I mean? Everyone wonders, if not sooner, then certainly later when there isn't much time left to be found. I wonder about it especially in December, when each morning I see the sun rise a little later and farther south, and set more murkily each late afternoon behind a shield of gray Ontario cloud. Its arc—when I can see it—hardly climbs above the bare branches of the topmost trees on Carmel Hill, which is both a companion and an image of my own "inner mountain" in my quiet Combermere poustinia.

The light is going, and I find myself busier than ever, caught up even here in the desert in that strange Advent haste that most North Americans call "the Christmas rush." I think we are all Einsteins, with our own theories of general and special relativity, particularly in December as light shrinks daily, and doors close.

> What freezings have I felt, what dark days seen!
> What old December's bareness every where![1]

It is the old age of the year, dark with the passage of time, busy with too many endings. Yet it is also Advent, and in our rush and haste we say to the great King who will come as a child, "Come!" and wonder what we mean.

We *do* what we mean. "Doing" isn't the only gauge of "meaning"; the human heart and the human act are both intricately subtle, and what you see is by no means necessarily what you get. There is always more than meets the eye. Yet play as many games of "knowing" as you want, you will, finally, come to the test that Christ himself proposed: "By their fruits you will know them" (Matt 7:20). In December we grasp for time and throw it away. We are getting ready for Christmas.

---

[1]William Shakespeare, Sonnet XCVII, ll. 3–4.

But who is this "we" that prepares Christmas so busily, and what is the fruit we seek? "We" can't really include all those who for whatever reason exclude themselves from Christmas. However, this is a real, social, cultural "we," embracing monk and mother, career woman and football player, suburbanite and urban poor, media persons and down-home folks, the powerful and the dispossessed, those who passionately yearn for the great King's coming and those who, with sighs, prepare to do another social duty. Our separate lives go on, but the communal we—for a time more like a family than a socio-economic system—spends itself in a carefully plotted frenzy of shopping, buying, cooking, partying, card-writing, eating and drinking, remembering, praying sometimes, and maybe even fasting. We look to children, who know how to hope for the fulfillment of a promise that thrills them just because it is bigger than anything they can understand or imagine. We find within us the place that hopes to be unimaginably surprised.

But still—are all of these December-Advent carryings-on cut from the same cloth? Aren't some secular and some spiritual, some Christian, some neopagan, and some just plain human "doings"? No doubt: but I am fascinated by our busyness, and my own, and by its occasion. We are getting ready for Christmas, for the great King's coming to be born in a cave in Bethlehem. If we look at his Mother, we see prayerful listening, quiet pondering on this Word who has taken her flesh and now fills her heart. Then why am I so busy? Why are you? Why so much urgency that even football—a secular liturgy if there ever was one—is caught up and molded by it?

Urgency: why not? After all, God, not Santa Claus, is coming to town. He is coming as a baby, and babies are meant to be made by love. Aren't all our carryings-on and rememberings ways of making love? And aren't we making it as the visible light of life daily lessens and darkness grows? Doesn't December force upon us the reality of time's passage—and its apparently irretrievable loss? Don't we look to Christmas, then, in several sorts of hope and spend our time ever faster and more prodigally, proposing to life and even to God, as Andrew Marvell did to his coy mistress, that

> . . . though we cannot make our sun
> Stand still, yet we will make him run?[2]

This is what we *do,* hoping to see new light at light's end and to find new time when time has run out. But do we really mean it? It all

---

[2]Andrew Marvell, "To His Coy Mistress," ll. 45–46.

depends, of course, on how seriously you take the sun. Now many of us would assume that this is a question of personal taste, varying with occupation, climate, season, and age. A sunny day is almost always welcome, but the sun itself—serious, even urgent?

Certainly in recent decades we have come to understand the sun's workings—and to fear their human reproduction. The sun, our star, is a thermonuclear furnace of such enormous mass that even though it has been burning up and sending out as light and energy millions of tons of itself *every second* for 4.5 billion years, it will continue to do so for at least another 4.5 billion years or so. That is awesome by human standards, but in the immensity that is the universe, the sun is merely one of some hundreds of billion stars in our own galaxy, which is one among hundreds of billion other galaxies, each of which contains similar numbers of stars. Still, in relation to us, as *our* sun, this thermonuclear mass is surely serious enough. It gives, or has given, or will give us everything we have and are and will be.

Physically. We are going deeper into the seriousness of the sun—because we are both physical and something more, and the sun has something to do with that something more. Listen to Henry Beston, for example:

> A year indoors is a journey along a paper calendar; a year in outer nature is the accomplishment of a tremendous ritual. To share in it, one must have a knowledge of the pilgrimages of the sun, and something of that natural sense of him and feeling for him which made even the most primitive people mark the summer limits of his advance and the last December ebb of his decline. . . . When all has been said, the adventure of the sun is the great natural drama by which we live, and not to have joy in it and awe of it, not to share in it, is to close a dull door on nature's sustaining and poetic spirit.[3]

Beston's sun is the splendid king of earth and sky whose royal pilgrimages make days and summers happen, whose calm withdrawals shape the seasonal beauty of the earth and the mystery of night. This sun is the master of ordinary time. If you close your eyes to him, you will lose more than poetry. You will never see the face of the earth, your mother.

But our ancestors, "primitive" in their greater closeness to our human origins but our elders and teachers in their awareness of what is more than physical, did not record the sun's comings and goings

[3]Henry Beston, *The Outermost House: A Year of Life on the Great Beach of Cape Cod* (New York: Ballantine Books, 1949; repr. from Holt, Rinehart and Winston, Inc., 1928), pp. 47–48.

either out of esthetic feeling or out of fear. They knew continuity when they saw it. They knew the sun had continuity – in its way. It came and went, but it always came back. They knew that they didn't have continuity. They saw that time passed, and for each of them it also ended. The reality of death drew them to a darker side of the sun, more elusive to the eye or mind. They saw their own discontinuity – death – reflected in the sun's unconquerable coming back, for they discovered that the sun brought them not only light and life, but also time and its passage, their own daily, yearly loss of it.

In this discovery our ancestors everywhere learned to make the first icon – the first human-fashioned embodiment of the invisible. This "icon" was not the sun itself, but an idea drawn from it, an inner image of transcendence: sacred time. Time would never stand still. For humans it would always end. But the sun's eternal return became a symbol – not of heaven exactly or even nirvana, certainly not of reincarnation or of resurrection – but of a time beyond time. This other "time," beyond the sun, would give humans a new way of being – gathering, not scattering, finding without losing. In it the stillness of death could also become an icon, the image of wholeness absolutely found. And once discovered, sacred time would transform natural time. Human life would be open to infinite possibility; each "now" could truly be the moment of beginning forever.

We may seem a long way from this December, and this Christmas coming, but it was then, when our ancestors began to understand the other side of the sun, that humans first began to prepare for Christmas. I always think of those ancestors as my mothers and fathers – Cro-Magnons etching antlers with the phases of the moon and descending into caves to paint splendid universes of animals; unnamed men and women fashioning tiny figures of the Great Mother to show their knowledge of the maternal wholeness of the earth, a sort of human, female sun; Egyptians and Chinese building vast monuments to carry them beyond solar time; unknown Cree shamans and African grandmothers telling stories of other worlds; dancers, astrologers, and priests seeking the rhythms and the speech of the masters and mistresses of sacred time; the original Australians dreaming themselves into its true geography; all the hunters and the growers so familiar with the visible world and thus so alert to the invisible; and even, later, the poets writing their disillusioned, elegant lyrics. All of them are my own mothers and fathers "longing for a better country" (Heb 11:16), pilgrims in search of rest.

But they didn't find it. Individuals did, no doubt, and even certain peoples may have, for a while, but if the collective voice of our ancestors could comment on Beston's "great natural drama" of the sun, it would pronounce that drama a tragedy. Too much suffering to be called comedy, too much earnestness for farce, humankind's pilgrimages with the sun, sacred or profane, have ended painfully, if often nobly, in a murk of gods and goddesses, on the ashheap of history, or simply in the darkness of death. Time always ran out.

Snow is falling outside in the graying light. It is covering the cold December earth. Let us draw closer to the fire. The sun is a king, and it seemed to promise something to hope for. But the sun is not the great King, and now the great King is coming. Let us be still together. Let us hear what this King has to say to all our mothers and fathers—and to us: "None of them received what had been promised. God had planned something better for us so that only together with us would they be made perfect" (Heb 11:39-40). The Epistle to the Hebrews is speaking especially of our Jewish ancestors in faith, but its words embrace all those who sought the invisible place where time became no longer repetition, but inexhaustible life. In the rush and bustle of Advent we become one with all our ancient mothers and fathers. Their carryings-on and ways of remembering, like ours, meant to make love happen. Like us, they hurried to the day when light was reborn. Let us be still together and listen for the name of this "something better" that God planned for us all.

Look at Buddha, the greatest of all those outside of Israel who knew that not all of creation, not any knowledge, nor sacred act, nor any god or goddess, could bring us to the moment of utter silence. Let us be silent with him. Look at Moses, the greatest of our prophets, who spoke to God "mouth to mouth, clearly" (Num 12:8), and received the words of his Covenant, but still did not see the full glory of the Lord, and was not allowed to enter the land of promise. Let us understand what he understood: that the Lord God alone made heaven and earth and all they contain; that he made the sun and the other lights to give light to the earth and "for signs and for seasons and for days and years" (Gen 1:14); that he created time and its passage, and also the Sabbath, Passover, and other seasonal feasts. God himself, then, the great King, made both time and history, and, as he walked and talked with Israel, both sacred time and sacred history.

But Christmas: God surprised everyone even more than when he called Abraham out of Ur, even more than when he took Israel out of Egypt and spoke to Moses on Mount Sinai, even more than when he gave the prophets shattering words to proclaim that the sacred history Israel shared with the Lord God would be fulfilled on that *day* – the end of even sacred history – when the King himself would come to reign over all the earth. Christmas: the first one, though all creation was there with Joseph, the angels, the shepherds, and the animals, was a quiet affair, an intimate concelebration of the Blessed Trinity and Mary. Now that I think of it, Mary's preparation had been busy enough – journeying to Elizabeth and back, setting up house with a man whose faith was second only to hers, traveling again, her body heavy with the Child, all the way to Bethlehem. But that night was quiet, I think, when the King's Son, himself King of kings and Lord of lords, came forth from her womb, when the Mother of God kissed her Son for the first time and made her first communion kneeling on the straw in a manger.

But Christmas still wasn't quite Christmas. It couldn't be until that Child had grown and gone forth to create another sort of communion, first in the upper room with his disciples, then on the cross with his blood, and finally, raised up, glorified, enthroned, and empowered to send the Holy Spirit through his transformed flesh into ours. The Christmas that we are getting ready for couldn't happen without the Church, and if we want to see the Church celebrating its first Christmas, we look to those gentle yet overwhelming meetings between the risen Christ and his friends, especially the meeting at Emmaus, where he opened the Scriptures to them, made himself known to them in the breaking of the bread, and filled their hearts with the same fire Moses had entered on Sinai.

We are almost there. It took the Church centuries to learn from the Holy Spirit in terms of human language, gesture, and ritual what the Lord Jesus had meant when he said, "Do this in memory of me" (Lk 22:19). The Eucharist itself, of course, was in a real sense everything that the Lord had left the Church; the followers of Jesus Christ came to know themselves too as his Body, enlightened by his Word, in the breaking of the bread each Sunday. Weekly Easter, yearly Easter, weekly vigils, morning praise, vespers, martyrs' days, first stirrings of Lent – the structure of the Church's liturgy unfolded simply in both East and West, though the battles over the dating of Easter reveal that the Church was still being taught by the Holy Spirit about the specific meaning of Christian time. But only when the Roman Empire bowed its head to Jesus Christ as its true Lord and God was the Church challenged to make fully public the implications of its faith. It proclaimed that faith at Nicea in 325, and some 30 years later it created something just as bold as the *homoousian* (the declaration in the Creed that Jesus is of one substance, one nature, with the Father): it seized the December celebration of the "unconquerable sun" and all the wild goings-on surrounding it, and claimed it for the birth of Jesus Christ, the world's true light.

Easter, and its yearly celebration, made quite clear the Christian conviction that the deepest work of the Kingdom had already been accomplished: Christ's own body had become the crucible in which our sin and our death were transformed into sacraments of God's love; now, glorified, Christ is King of all times and ages. But this feast we call in English, "Christ-mass," (and its Eastern twin, Epiphany) would link forever the enfleshing of the Eternal Light and the natural drama of the sun. The Holy Spirit was giving us eyes to see that the journey we make around the sun every 365 days is a sacrament, in its depths an inner pilgrimage within the mystery hidden from all eternity in God and made known in the human, broken, and Spirit-filled flesh of Jesus, our servant-king. We have entered the inner life of God, and all the moments we lose or even waste we rediscover—made whole; made immortal—within the merciful heart of the God who has come to live on our earth, in our flesh, in our time, in our hearts.

Christmas is coming, and we are trying as fast as we can to get there. We are trying to remember the story and fill it with as much love as we can find so that our children will understand it and love the Child who is welcoming them with so much love; so that the child within too will let the Child console her, console him. Because that Child has all the time in the world. For him all the time between his resurrection and his second coming—all of that "already but not yet" we know so well—is for him time found. For us it may still be loose change waiting to be added to the treasure of the Kingdom by faith and love, odds and ends of days, years, lives, and especially the "waste" of suffering, still needing to be immersed in the unending offering of Christ to the Father. But in joyfully and humbly showing himself to us as the Child year after year, Jesus shows us that he has all the time in the world. What we've lost, he's found, and he is happy to wait for us to bring him the rest of what we've got so that he can share with us the banquet of all that he has—the everlasting banquet of love.

The whole human family is gathering around the manger. It's a little crowded; there's a bit of pushing and shoving, and some of the cousins are far from friendly. Many won't arrive for quite some time. Surely we need to try again to tell them—show them—what we've found here: truly something better, the Child who takes whatever we have to offer and returns to us the gift of the Trinity's absolutely still and infinitely unrepetitive exchange of love. Since they might not understand that, it would certainly be best to show them by doing it ourselves. But anyway, right now at least we're doing it as well as we can. We're here, aren't we? Isn't it good that we found time?

WHO IS THIS WOMAN?

There was a moment when all of creation held its breath and waited for a young Jewish girl to speak. It was a moment within time, a definite minute on a definite day in a definite year, as the earth spun around the sun and the sun wheeled in its galactic orbit, as kings prepared for war and villagers went about their chores. It was also a moment embracing all time, from the Word that called the very first morning forth to the last syllable that will wholly transfigure both heaven and earth.

As the minister of God's light waited in amazement to hear what the girl would say, for an instant all the angels ceased their praises, were still, and waited with him. The world felt itself hanging on her word. The voices of the earth were hushed. Animals paused, their instincts telling them that their lives too hung in the balance. Birds hovered and fell silent, as during an eclipse. The great currents of water and air hesitated, so that whales and minnows alike, seedlings and oaks all turned toward Nazareth. Even the demons grew silent, and did not know what to think. All across the world, in the quiet that comes when even the breath is momentarily still, every human ear strained to hear the beating of a single heart, a young Jewish girl's heart. God himself waited for her to speak. Who is she?

I know her name. I know what word she breathed into that silence, the world's and God's, and I know what Word God breathed into her silence. But who is she?

She was not a conscious part of my childhood. I cannot remember what cold December she first became for me part of the Christmas story. In the churches I went to there were no pictures of her, no statues, probably not even a creche at Christmas. Her name was never mentioned, not even, I think, the time we were told in Sunday school that the Catholics who worshiped in the church across the street from ours prayed to idols.

Yet we loved Christmas too, and as I think of that, I realize that it isn't accurate to say that the name of this woman before whom even God once held his breath was never spoken in our church. We too listened to the great Gospel of Christmas: "Now in that day there went out a decree from Caesar Augustus that all the world should be taxed. . . ." Even now I can hear her name falling softly through the candle-lit night into my heart. Who did I think she was? I don't know, really. I only knew that she was the mother who "gave birth to her first-born son and wrapped him in swaddling clothes, and laid him in a manger because there was no room for them in the inn."

But I remember that we sang of her too, that one night of the year, that magic night, that silent night when the whole world seemed to be waiting as eagerly as my brother and I were for some marvelous surprise: "All is calm, all is bright,/'Round yon Virgin Mother and Child." I remember how many times I sang that lovely carol as a child, and I cannot say if I wondered who she was, this Virgin, this Mother. Still, when I think of those words, and when I remember those Christmases, a light so gently radiant surrounds them that it seems to me that she must have smiled at me, even though I never saw that smile until so much later.

Much later, I bought my first rosary. It was a difficult time for me, a time when I was struggling to find both God and my own adult self. I remember the shop I went to, and I realize now that as I crossed that street in New Haven, I was traveling a far vaster distance than the one between two curbs. Even then, though, I sensed that I was passing some hidden frontier. I wanted a small crucifix to keep in my pocket, but it wasn't the buying of a crucifix that made me step warily into that shop, carrying my late adolescent cool like some fragile egg that might crack at the slightest misstep in this foreign land. I didn't know this woman whose beads I was buying, but I felt, I think, that I was arranging a secret meeting with her that I would have to keep.

On Christmas Eve of that same year I lit my first candle in front of her image. After the service in our little Methodist church, I slipped across the street to the church that had always been alien ground. It didn't seem so foreign that night despite the smell of incense and candles that hung beneath the gilded wooden rafters. It wasn't home yet, either. It was simply a place where prayers were offered and heard, and that Christmas Eve as I lit that small vigil light, I asked the silent woman whose name I scarcely knew to pray that I might come safely through the darkness inside me to the place where her Son wanted me.

She did, and I did. On the night of Easter light three months later as I prepared to come home to the fullness of her Son's Church, I knew that she had led me to him. I took a new name that night, a French priest's name that included her name, because I knew that her love had watched over and guided me. I still didn't know who she was, but as I fell asleep after our feast, her name sounded like a great bell in my heart. I had begun to know that she was my Mother as well as Christ's.

After that great Easter of my rebirth, I have a thousand memories of her. Images of her crowd my heart—pictures, statues, ideas, experiences, moments of silent communion beyond either language or imagination. I was a member now of a family that belonged to her, and she was never far away. Her feasts gave me joy. Her presence beside me at each station of the cross consoled me. The scenes of her rosary shaped my faith so deeply that even when I stopped reciting it every day, her silence continued to comfort me with the knowledge of God's coming in our flesh.

I was ordained priest on the Feast of her Queenship, on the day that later became the Feast of the Visitation, but it is only now, many years later, that I begin to realize how truly she had visited me that day to make it another kind of Christmas for me. It was another song, a song several worlds away from "Silent Night," that God used to begin to form this awareness within me. One evening I sat in Fr. Eddie's room, watching television with him. I was not lost or unhappy or rebellious, only—as I look back at it now—beginning to understand the coldness of my heart, the frailty of my certitudes, the real depth of the mystery of my life and something of its unfathomability. Then, suddenly, the Beatles were singing about this woman, a Mother, coming through the darkness to speak a single word of wisdom, "Let it be." "Let it be," she said to me. "Let it be." And when I discovered later that the Beatles may have thought they were singing about another mother and another comfort, I didn't care. I knew that there was only one Mother who could teach my heart how to say "*Fiat*": "let it be for me and in me, God, as you want, as you say." I began to understand, a little, of what it means to be held.

She gave me more than her word that night. She shared with me her stillness. Who is she, this Jewish woman, that she can walk through a television set into a slowly hardening, middle-aging heart? I do not know. I only know that the following spring, as I tried to apply what she'd taught me to a time of rectory warfare, she came to me again. Again she came suddenly, but this coming was like the midwestern spring itself—surprising, warm, ecstatic. She came to me like Easter. As I prayed one April day, I felt the brightness of her joy burst over me so vividly that I turned with a start, thinking I might see her there, right by my shoulder, so strongly did I feel her love. A season of glad songs had come. For weeks I sensed her closeness, anointing me, bathing me in a joy so huge, so simple, so immaculate that each day I became a child again, ready to be amazed anew by the marvels of heaven and earth.

Who is she, this mother of all joy? I never was able to catch sight of her with my bodily eyes, yet I know that I caught for the first time a little of her fragrance, the sweetness of spring after a very long winter. I knew that she was the mother of my own risen body already being knitted together in the womb of her love.

But who she is, this Mother of the resurrection, I still cannot say, even though since that spring she has come to live with me in a new way. Since then, the Father has put some of his children into my own heart, and she has enabled the Spirit to teach me what little I know about letting him reveal the face of Jesus within them. Since then, in a moment of anguish I plunged through all the fear still left within me, only to discover to my great astonishment a trust in her even more real than my own body, a trust that began to enable me, at long last, to hear the words of love her Son was speaking to me.

Once I heard with the ears of my spirit the song of praise she sings to the Father, a song filling heaven and earth, simpler than light, more constant than gravity. With my inner eye I have at times caught a glimpse of her. Once she was more splendid than all the galaxies hurtling themselves into a single explosion of glory. Sometimes she is standing at the foot of the Cross, leaning forward in such a communion of pain that I wonder again who this woman is that the Word of God chose her to will with him our rebirth. But usually when the eyes of my faith see her, she is looking at one of her children and mine. Her face is so filled then with tenderness, so radiant in her love, that my heart would break with joy even if she didn't then look at me too, to smile at me for loving as best I can these beloved ones of hers and Christ's. And once, in a little Mexican church at the very end of a long road, she spoke a word of love straight from her heart into mine.

Who is this woman? I cannot say. I only know that Christmas is coming again. It is time again for the Cross to be transformed into the glorious, evergreen tree of life that it truly is, time again for the songs and the food that tell us that heaven has come to earth. It is time again for the Child to teach us that childhood is not past, but future, and if we want, right now. It is time again for this woman to make us understand that the place where she gives this child birth is the cave of our own hearts.

Christmas is coming, and when I think of this woman, I think of the words Fr. Eddie spoke to Catherine one day not too long before he died. "I can't tell you," he said, "how much you have meant to me. I can only say that you have brought beauty into my life. You have brought love into my life. You have brought God into my life." I cannot say who this woman is, the Mother of my Lord, this woman who is my mother, my sister, my joy. But I know that she has brought beauty and joy into my life—and faith and love. I know that she has brought God into my life. I know that she has put all the children of God into my heart. I know that she has taught me how to love Jesus. I know that I love her.

Most of the world is still waiting for Christmas. Birds still pause in the air, and oaks and minnows still turn toward Nazareth. The angels continue to look at this woman in wonder, and even now the demons do not know what to think. Most human hearts are still confused and frightened, and some turn to her blindly, ignorantly, waiting for her word. But God is not silent and breathless any longer. The woman has spoken, and God has spoken, and together for all eternity they will go on speaking the Word made flesh, the word of life: Jesus. I do not know how to say who she is, but I know that I love her. What is more important, I do know how to say her name, "Mary," and I know that she loves me.

GOD REST YOU MERRY

Days of light, days of mild warmth: this year is fading away like a happy old man, mellow with love, delighted to find out that the final letting-go is such a joy. There is still winter to face, of course, but the fragrance, however faint, of peace in the air, and these sun-tinged December days hint at a spring that lies months away. As bright day follows clear night, at the very center of my mind and growing more vivid by the hour is the image of an infant, gently waving his arms and kicking his feet in the air. He seems alone in the darkness, even though I sense the whole universe watching him with me, because his body, as in Caravaggio's magnificent "Deposition," catches and holds all light, created and uncreated. He is the true light shining in the darkness, and the darkness cannot overcome him. He is Jesus.

Hardly strange, perhaps: who would you expect to find at the center of a Madonna House priest-poustinik's mind? Besides, the new television shows are much the same as last year's, football is hobbling toward the Bowls, hockey and basketball have begun again, while in the real world light dwindles, and we have entered the vigil of Advent. Of course I am thinking of the baby Jesus.

Yes, of course—and yet the way that baby focuses my mind is not a matter of course. I am not thinking about him, nor even imagining him. Rather, I have found his image present at the center of my consciousness, like the gift that every baby is, especially this one. Paddling there serenely in his own pure light, he is surely the answer to some question I scarcely knew I was asking. What was it?

"Blessed are the pure of heart: they shall see God" (Matt 5:8) and not the cluttered pawnshop that passes in most of us for a mind. But the question I'm looking for—the one whose answer is the flesh of God's Word—can't be too hard to find. Mind-questions clutter the brain, usually because they are second-hand and not worth claiming, sometimes because greed priced them far beyond the few pennies they were worth. But heart-questions, now they rise in the mind as simple, silent, and individual as stars and wait there peacefully, if they are allowed, until they are answered.

So then, when I put it to myself like that, I know at once what my heart is asking: how do I *be?* Or, in other words, what is Christmas? Or, put still differently, where is glory? You probably get it, and if you do, you might want to read something else or say some prayers; but then again, you might want to find out why I am asking myself such questions in the first place.

Well, I think that it all goes back—actually, it goes all the way back to my own babyhood, and to the world's, but that is not just another story; that is the whole story—to a question that the Lord Jesus put in my heart over a year ago: "Who is keeping you out of the kingdom?" I had two answers to that question. The first was that I knew very well who was *not* keeping me out of the Kingdom, and the second was that I was simply going to have to let the question sit in my heart until the Spirit told me how to answer it. The answers to the questions Jesus asks have their own gestation periods, and there is no use complaining about morning-sickness.

So I let the question gestate. I must admit that, as the months went by, I was tempted often to give the obvious answer: me! But each time I listened to that answer, I heard the counterfeit clank of self-accusation, not the ring of the Lord's own life-giving word. For once in my life I waited, not passionately like Job, not patiently like Mary, not even realizing too clearly that I was pregnant. I simply waited.

Then one quiet Saturday night, as I read a commentary on Ephesians, the waters broke. The Spirit spoke through St. Paul's words:

> But God loved us with so much love that he was generous with his mercy: when we were dead through our sins, he brought us to life with Christ—it is by grace that you have been saved—and raised us up with him and seated us with him in heaven, in Christ Jesus. This was to show for all ages to come, through his goodness toward us in Christ Jesus, how infinitely rich he is in grace. Because it is by grace that you have been saved, through faith; not by anything of your own, but by a gift from God; not by anything that you have done, so that nobody can claim the credit. We are God's work of art, created in Christ Jesus to live the good life as from the beginning he had meant us to live it (Eph 2:4–10).

I had been, I saw, chosen in Christ to live through love in God's presence; had been freely given my freedom through Christ's blood;

had died with Christ and had been raised with him and was seated at the Father's right hand in glory. It had already happened. I was in the Kingdom, lifted beyond the stars, that I might be filled with the fullness of him who fills all creation. Yes, I said, yes; God has won. The Father has done it all, the Son has done it all, the Spirit has done it all. My part is simply faith: to say yes. I said yes.

Oh, I saw the objections, but I knew that this was not fideism or quietism. I saw that, as St. Paul said, I must still "run to capture the prize for which Christ Jesus captured me" (Phil 3:12). I saw that only hope and love, the fruit of the gift of faith as we wait, groaning with all creation, would enable the Lord "to transform these lowly bodies of ours so that they will be like his glorious body" (Phil 3:21). I saw that I needed to pray daily, every moment, for the Spirit to enlighten my heart and strengthen my hidden self to know and to grasp the fullness of Christ's love. But I saw that I ran, hoped, loved, and prayed *within* the Kingdom. I was at home in my Father's house. He had unveiled my face to reflect the brightness of the Lord, and I had only to choose at each instant "to grow brighter and brighter as [I was] being turned into the image" (2 Cor 3:18) that I reflected.

Rest: it was rest Jesus was offering me—and all those who would lay down the burdens of their own projects to accept the easy yoke of becoming with him a child of God. Rest—as T. S. Eliot called it, "a condition of complete simplicity/(Costing not less than everything)."[1] And so I rested in glory—and watched with amazement what Jesus could do without my running interference for him.

It was then that the real objection to the Gospel hit me. Not the accusation of cowardice or irresponsibility or passivity; I knew that believing in the victory of Jesus would be the hardest work I'd ever undertaken. Not the horrors of the world's pain or the stench of my own sins; at last I might be able to do something practical about them. Not even the awful slowness with which the yeast of the risen Jesus was transforming the universe into good bread. No, the real objection was simpler, more fundamental: how could I rest and enjoy what I had not earned? How could the Kingdom be my home if it were "only" a gift? And with that I understood how Adam and Eve had thrown away Paradise—and what I had inherited from them. We are capable of Auschwitz and Hiroshima and the Gulag, of everyday cruelty and unspeakable crime because what we call life is death. We refuse true being. We *be* wrong.

[1]T. S. Eliot, "Little Gidding," *Four Quartets. The Complete Poems and Plays: 1909-1950* (New York: Harcourt, Brace and Company, 1952), p. 145.

For the last while, then, as the year has let go with such gentle grace, my heart has answered the question of Jesus with my own question: how do I *be* "yes"? The word the Spirit is offering me in reply is no human word, but the Word of God in the flesh, in baby-flesh. As I lean forward in the darkness to watch him – now playing, now resting in the light – I wonder how long it will be before my heart turns into the image of the one whom I reflect. Does it matter when faith shows you how his light is already gleaming on his Mother's face – and how they smile at each other? It is good to be here in this place of rest, in this place of glory, to wait for the smile on God's human face to fill the whole universe, and our hearts too, with the sheer delight of freely given infinite love.

A MEDITATION ON THE INFANT'S SMILE

There is in man an eternal element, a "germ of eternity," which already "breathes the upper air". . . . The truth of his being evades his being itself. For he is made in the image of God, and in the mirror of his being the Trinity is ever reflected. But it is only a mirror, an image. If man, by an act of sacrilege, inverts the relationship, usurps God's attributes, and declares that God was made to man's image, all is over with him. . . . Only by acknowledging himself to be a reflection could he obtain completeness, and only in his act or adoration could he find his own inviolable depths. Henceforth, then, he is estranged from himself, *dispersed*, separated from himself, and far more grievously and fundamentally than in Marx's description![1]

On the wall of our chapel there hangs an image of the Infant Christ. He is wrapped in swaddling clothes, his body completely hidden except for his face. His eyes are shut, and his lips curve in a smile of utter peace. "Truly, I say to you, unless you turn and become like children, you will never enter the kingdom of heaven" (Matt 18:3). The smile of the Infant holds the secret of everlasting life.

I love that image, and I never leave the chapel without kissing it and asking Christ to share his secret with me. But sometimes when I look at this Infant, I remember a story I read long ago. A certain captured Crusader and his Muslim jailer had each learned enough of the other's language to speak together of their lives and of those deep differences that had so ironically brought them together. One day as they talked, the Muslim said, "But who is your God that you speak of the place where he was born and the place where he died?"

Shyly, the Crusader said, "I'll show you." He reached under his tunic and brought out a small wooden image of Christ held in the

---

[1]Henri de Lubac, *Catholicism: A Study of Dogma in Relation to the Corporate Destiny of Mankind*, trans. Lancelot Sheppard (New York: Sheed & Ward, 1958), p. 199.

arms of his Mother. The Crusader pointed to the Infant and said, "There! That is God!"

The Muslim looked at his captive in horror. "A baby? Your God is a baby?"

There it is: the scandal of the Gospel. Nothing ever removes it completely. The theologian can qualify, the iconographer depict, the historian fill in context, the mystic call to mystery. Still the outrageous meeting of babyhood and Godhead presents itself—beyond all qualification, portrayal, historical context, and even intimate experience—for simple acceptance or rejection. As secret and as elusive as the Infant's smile, the Incarnation is at once too big and too tiny to grasp. Only the saints, who let that meeting truly happen in their own flesh, reveal how such scandalous news is good.

The saints, like the finely-polished mirrors of gigantic telescopes, catch and focus a light that the naked eye cannot see. But the light that the saints catch is not like starlight, too distant to see. It is as if, in enfleshing the Light of lights, they mirror the sun itself, its light too fiery for our direct gaze and too ordinary when seen indirectly to praise sensibly. That is Christmas—to see the invisible light made visible and to know that the Eternal One has made his home in human hearts.

The Church gives us Christmas not as a substitute for sanctity, others' or our own, but to enable us to see and taste and feel and hear and smell, even if only for a few days, the new world that began to be born when God himself was born in Bethlehem. At Christmas we discover that childhood is not so far from us as we supposed. We touch our own deepest humanity and, consciously or not, find there what the saints find: a splendid reflection that brings us wholeness, a bowing down that lifts us into heaven, a reconciliation beyond all our many alienations, a home that we have often thought we can never come to. We are no longer strangers, peering in at the windows of others, wondering where might be the tenderness that would welcome us, out of the dark and cold, into the warm, bright feast. We are beloved children at home around the table, and we know the secret of the Infant's smile of peace.

Is the scandal, then, left behind, a remnant of extraordinary ignorance that crumbles away in the dawning of the truly ordinary light of Christmas? Not yet; not yet. The Infant's smile scandalizes for the same reason that the cry of anguish torn from the full-grown and crucified Jesus, swaddled this time in pain and blood and loneliness, scandalizes. Each images the other, and each proclaims the foolishness of a God who is, incredibly, at the mercy of those whose agony is that they do not know mercy.

Of what use are this baby's smile and this man's cry? Can they feed the hungry or clothe the naked? Can they break the yoke of oppression and set the poor free? Can they answer the questions of the learned, or calm the fears of the terrified, create just economic systems, heal neurosis, bring back from the dead the victims of violence from Abel to the children of Kampuchea or the prisoners of the Lubyanka? And if the smile and the cry are of no tangible use, then is not our sense of being brought safely home by them simply a dangerous illusion?

We begin to see, to grasp both Christmas and Easter, when we reverse each image and discover that still they reflect each other. For the man who had been naked spoke again, after he had carried the omnipotent power of merciful love into the heart of death itself: "Mary . . . Simon son of John . . . I will be with you all days: peace." And the baby who smiled rested, not in the lap of luxury, but on the lap of love. We step back and look, and we see that he is lying in a stable, a cave, and that from the very beginning he had nowhere to lay his head – except on the breast of that woman whose love imaged Love itself. We step back again and see that the stable is an out-of-the-way village in a conquered land, the child himself a stranger, soon to be an exile, rumored among his own people to be illegitimate.

When Jesus was circumcised, God himself was marked in the flesh by the intimacy of his covenant with Israel. As the All-powerful became visibly vulnerable, he marked our inmost hearts with the truth that the "Most High" is most near. In becoming powerless, he embraced the powerlessness that lies at the heart of all pain. It seemed to hold no promise, to be absolutely nothing at all. Then he touched it with infant hands, with pierced hands, with dead hands, with risen hands, and that very nothing became a seed of unconquerable life.

> Nothing is more superficial than the charge made against [the Church] of losing sight of immediate realities, of neglecting man's urgent needs, by speaking to him always of the hereafter. For in truth the hereafter is far nearer than the future, far nearer than what we call the present. It is the Eternal found at the heart of all temporal development which gives it life and direction. It is the authentic Present without which the present itself is like the dust which slips through our hands. If modern men are so *absent* from each other, it is

primarily because they are absent from themselves, since they have abandoned this Eternal which alone establishes them in being and enables them to communicate with one another.[2]

And so we come home at Christmas, home to a childhood lovelier than our sweetest memory, home to an adulthood more splendid than our best hope, home to our own hearts, home to the hearts of others, brothers and sisters now, and friends, home to our own world, home to the Eternal who loves us so much that he has made his home with us. We need no longer absent ourselves from home, out of fear, out of pride, out of misguided concern for those who seem even farther away than we. Even they are waiting for us at the place where we finally become humble enough to admit that we have been made for joy. "Come," they say, "and share your joy with us." "Come home to us," our brothers and sisters say. The saints too in their radiance say to us, "Come!" And the lovely one, the Mother of us all, the new Eden where the Father recreated man, she too says, "Come home." The Infant smiles and welcomes us, and promises to teach us that secret of love by which we too can give our lives so that the whole world can one day celebrate Christmas.

The scandal is transformed at last – beyond paradox, even beyond gentle irony – into something as simple and as mysterious as marriage. And if you listen to the songs we sing as we gather round the table, you will know that they will be sung some day on the farthest planet of the farthest star of the farthest galaxy in the universe, as everything that breathes rejoices in the embrace of God.

---

[2]*Ibid.*, p. 201.

THE NAME OF JESUS

"On the eighth day, when it was time to circumcise him, he was named Jesus, the name the angel had given him before he had been conceived" (Lk 2:21).

Who said it first, after Gabriel I mean? Surely Mary did. Joseph must have spoken the child's name to the rabbi on the day of the circumcision, but it must have been Mary who first named her child "Jesus." Perhaps it was in that instant when the air was just coming back to itself, still ringing with the angel's presence and her own yes — her hand on her womb, her lips and her tongue echoing her heart. Perhaps it was when Joseph came to see her after the angel appeared to him in a dream. "And then," he would have said, "the angel told me that his name will be. . . ." "Jesus," Mary would have answered. "Yes, I know." Or did she wait until he first stirred in her body, and say his name then, at that moment when her baby began silently to speak, in wonder to find her own flesh somehow at the very center of life. Somehow: she wouldn't have known just how, and how carefully she and Joseph would have listened to be able to pronounce his name just so, never in vain, when the only cloud of glory proclaiming his presence was a young Jewish girl's pregnant womb.

"What's in a name?" Juliet asked. "That which we call a rose, by any other name would smell as sweet; so Romeo would, were he not Romeo called." You have to remember that she was very young, head over heels in love, and not likely to have thought through the absurdity of dying with the name "Federico" or "Giancarlo" on her lips, not to speak of "Achille" or "Amintore." Of course these names have their own virtues, but that is just the point. Though many philosophers and linguists, more intellectual if almost certainly less eloquent than Shakespeare's Juliet, might agree with her, the old commonsensical certitude that each thing and each person has just the name that speaks forth its true essence is becoming, with all due scholarly reservations, respectable again among intellectuals. It was the scientific study of structures and languages that first cast doubt on the old certitude, but that same study, prolonged now for hundreds of years, begins to approach the point our ancestors reached so long ago that they took it for granted: that to name something, and especially someone, is to see so keenly into its or her or his heart through the miracle of language that to change that name, or even to translate it, is to transform its very being by transforming its (or hers or his) relationship with everything else.

Our ancestors in faith, the Jews, knew this better than any other people. Other nations named their chief god or High God or divinity, but the Jews were never in danger of thinking that the Lord who had spoken to Moses out of the burning bush was by any other name – Brahman, Nyame, nhialic, or even (God forbid!) Moloch or Jupiter Capitolinus – the very same Y----h who had called them to be his unique people and to hear his own Name for himself. The name reveals the person, and how could the Jews ever forget this when they had come to know their own bridal name, Israel, in their ages-long wrestling with the One who was so far beyond all gods and all the names of gods that he dared to plunge into the bloody flux of human history to woo and win them as if he had no more self-regard than any moon-struck Romeo?

The name reveals the person: the name is the person. Because the Jews were told the unutterably mysterious Name by the unutterably mysterious One himself, they knew that they were called to *know* him, to be united to him in absolute intimacy, to be holy as he alone is holy, to love him with all their heart and all their soul and all their mind and all their strength. And because they knew that the Name was the Person and that their own name was their true being, they sang, "My heart has said of you, 'Seek his face,' it is your face, O Y----h, I seek" (Ps 27:8). As God's people sought the face of their beloved in every word that he had spoken, as they longed to realize with all their flesh and spirit the name he had given them, they saw too that they were not simply "they": each of them had a unique name, a face, a way of being. They began to understand why, no matter how dimly at first, the Lord's second great commandment, "Love your neighbor as yourself" (Deut 6:5), was like the first.

Of course they did not understand it perfectly as we Christians do not after 2000 years of proclaiming God's name in our flesh. God's people were so overwhelmed when the Name they had adored for all those centuries became a fully human name that they closed their ears in horror to the flesh that is their everlasting joy. But not "they," really: what do we do when we shrug away our angry brother's name at the altar or return his slap with one of our own if not reject the Name that the angel made known to Mary? And absolutely not "they" when you stop to think about it a little: who first spoke God's name in the flesh if not a young Jewish girl? Mary: only she can teach us, who were once not a people at all but are now grafted onto God's people, to speak this name so purely that we can say it not merely in the desert but before the burning bush of every human face.

"A person who experiences another person experiences immortality, and enters a mode of existence not bound by time or space or by any other condition," Archbishop Joseph Raya has written. "The encounter of a person is supreme beatitude, a feast."[1] These words summarize the rationale behind the Archbishop's version of the Eastern churches' "Office of the Name of Jesus." Our age—technocratic, bureaucratic, depersonalized, cut adrift from old moorings of place and family and worship—is obsessed with the desire for intimacy. Everyone is on a first-name basis with everyone else, including God. The craters on the dark side of the moon and galaxies beyond the reach of light-gathering telescopes have received at last their human names. Yet in this very spree of name-giving the old names for common things—flowers, birds, parents, saints—are forgotten or derided, and the passion for intimacy ends so often in a heartbreaking collection of "relationships." To dare to call the experience of one person by another an experience of immortality, we must again learn to say the Name that weds God's life and ours with the same care that Mary used, and uses, to say it. If I want to enter a "supreme beatitude" when I meet another, our meeting must bear witness to the Kingdom, present right here and now, that the Lord Jesus promised to everyone who received him, and all others, with the heart of a child.

God, not Karl Marx, was the first to recognize that overcoming alienation, all forms of estrangement, was the path to healing every human wound, even death. God restored the life that is blessed intimacy—by calling and renaming Abraham, by revealing his Name to Moses, by making Israel his bride, and, finally, by sharing with all peoples the mystery of his own inner life as he sent his eternal Word to dwell forever in our flesh. This One, God with God for all

---

[1] *The Eyes of the Gospel* (Denville, N.J.: Dimension Books, 1978), p. 22.

ages, was proclaimed Jesus by the angel, by Mary, and then publicly by the shedding of his blood. He spoke all that God is to us, and when we – not just "the Jews" but all of us – could not bear to meet such life, he embraced our death as well. When his Father raised him, he transformed the web of all our estrangements into an endless dance of life, a feast of meeting held forever in his own boundless meeting with the Father in the Holy Spirit.

> He, being in very nature God, did not consider equality with God something to be clung to, but emptied himself, taking the nature of a servant, being made in human likeness. And being found in appearance as a man, he humbled himself and became obedient to death – even death on a cross. Therefore God exalted him to the highest place and gave him the name that is above every name, that at the name of Jesus every knee should bow, in heaven and on earth and under the earth, and every tongue confess that Jesus Christ is Lord to the glory of God the Father (Phil 2:6–11).

This is what it means to proclaim that Jesus is Lord: not only that the Messiah of God has freed us from all bondage, not only that this Jew from Nazareth is King of the universe, but that his human name – "Jesus" – has become both the way home and home itself for all creation, the place of meeting for every person. But this name, given to us by the free grace of the Spirit, unmerited, unwon, unearned, must still be learned, even as Mary, who received it in the totality of her being, learned it as she pondered it in her heart. However others learn it, we who have already come to know the face of Jesus, the crucified and risen Messiah, who have received his life in baptism, fed on him in the Eucharist, and know him as our Lord and our God – we learn to say his name in countless ways: in the liturgy, in Scripture, from Mary and the saints, in the duty of every moment, and above all by opening ourselves in love to every person with whom this Lord of ours has identified himself – that is, to everyone.

Yet in some special way each Christian is called to meet Jesus and to learn his name by entering that secret place where he has already met us and speaks our own name. There, within, our mothers and fathers in faith learned to know Jesus as his Mother does, at the very time when the victory of the cross over Roman paganism had so revealed the utter holiness of the name of Jesus that it could hardly be spoken in ordinary speech. There, in the solitude and darkness where all meeting begins, we can ponder his name, speak it, sing it, weep it until the moment when Jesus chooses to show us his face, and our endless feast begins.

We may do whatever we want with the name, with one exception: we may not ignore it. That is a choice that is not given to us any more than it was given to Mary. We can, of course, do our worst and try to ignore it. We can yawn or curse or turn our backs. God will let us, because his name lives in only freely offered hearts, but he will never let us plead ignorance.

Does this mean that only devoted Christians will enter the kingdom? I think not: "I was hungry, and you fed me. . . ." "When, Lord?" "Whatever you did . . . , you did to me." "I was hungry and you did not feed me." "When, Lord?" "Whatever you did not do . . . , you did not do for me" (Matt 25:31*ff*). To ignore the name of Jesus, then, is to reject the Person who has identified himself with the person of even the least of his sisters and brothers. It is to refuse the way of the one who is love. It is to pull back from the Lord's gift of his blood and his Spirit—and to walk away from the feast into eternal isolation.

But think again of the one who first chose to learn how to speak the name of Jesus. Her "yes" let the face of the God no one can see and live shine on every human face that has come into the world. We wonder how to end the arms race, but will we learn the name of Jesus? We groan in fury and in terror over nuclear proliferation, but will we learn how to let Mary and the Spirit teach us the name of Jesus? We weep or rage over the state of the Church, but is the name that is truth and love beating in our hearts? Abortion, poverty, pleasure-worship, joblessness, the suffering of the young, the married, the old, our friends' coldness or our enemies' heat, decadent capitalism or satanic communism: how we complain and struggle, work and even pray, but, do we care enough to give our whole life to the name of Jesus, which is "far above all rule and authority, power and dominion, and every name that can be given, not only in the present age but also in the age to come" (Eph 2:21)?

Perhaps you try. Of course you try, as I do. But we can do better than try. We can go to Nazareth, the one inside, the place of stillness, and ask Mary and Joseph to teach us all they know. We can ask the Father and the Holy Spirit, who abide with us always, to teach us what we will never even begin to finish knowing. We can ask Jesus himself to make our names synonyms for his. Then whatever we see or touch or live or love will be blessedness itself. It will be enough. It will be all.

THE FEAST OF ENLIGHTENMENT: EPIPHANY AND THEOPHANY

The Age of Enlightenment is hastening to its end. In a clamor of propaganda, ideology, and lies, night is falling on the eighteenth-century dream of the autonomous human reason. The new day of mankind come of age—prophesied by Descartes, proclaimed by Voltaire, articulated by Kant and Hegel, carried to the nations by Marx and Lenin, made respectable by Darwin, and interiorized by Freud—that new day has grown old. It is dying in an agony of cynicism and astrology, in a growing paralysis of democratic materialism, socialist authoritarianism, and mindless revolution for its own sake. Much will not disappear, of course: scientific discoveries, medical miracles, political hopes, technological ingenuity, historical and psychological consciousness, dreams of individual worth and liberty. But the modern world is modern no longer. Its light is fading, and wherever one looks, at those who chant mantras or at those who used to quote Mao, one sees the blind groping for a new light.

Probably it is no accident that both mantras and Mao promise light from the East. In the lands of the morning sun, the children of the West look for the dawn. Even one of the greatest geniuses of our culture, whose mind is wholly French and altogether atheist, sees in the Buddha, the Enlightened One, the symbol of that illusionless compassion that alone makes the human march toward certain death bearable. No doubt Claude Lévi-Strauss has created a secularized Buddha, yet it is striking that the great Indian's wisdom still shines for him, but not that of Jesus or even Moses. Much of the West has lost confidence in the light of the unaided human mind. It has forgotten why such confidence seemed so well-placed for so long, and now, forgetting too the source of its own humanism, the grace of Christ, it looks for a new light, which is more than human, but not quite divine.

The enlightenment experienced and taught by the Buddha is one such light. He discovered that at the root of all suffering, especially the suffering of endless death and rebirth, lay desire. He found that the death of desire led a man past the illusion of a self that must be desired into existence to a state of new freedom so transcendent that one can only say of it that it neither is nor is not, that it is not both being and non-being nor is it neither. Such paradoxical language points to the perfect silence of Buddhist enlightenment, where the separateness of each creature is experienced in a timeless moment of absolute oneness. Thus the masters of Buddhist life seek to bring their disciples to this total emptiness in which is found both freedom and true power to alleviate suffering.

Yet it seems clear to me that neither the debased Buddhism that was Maoism nor the modernized versions of other Indian spiritualities can bring the West – or the world – the light it longs for. The reason is not the debasement or the modernization, but rather the hidden memory of another, still purer enlightenment. This memory, which reaches back to Abraham and is embodied in Jesus, has not been forgotten so much as it has, in the most literal sense, been repressed. It lies somewhere beneath the surface of the modern mind, its power diverted into a hundred different secular and religious channels, its life-creating beauty turned to poison by the very act of denial which this "forgetting" has been.

And what have we forgotten? That the light which enlightens every man and woman who comes into the world has itself come into the world, and the darkness of the world could not overcome it (cf. Jn 1:3–5). That the uncreated light has become visible in the flesh of Jesus Christ, who was born of the Virgin Mary. That he who is the world's light has penetrated to the very heart of darkness, has risen, and shines now forever in all of those who go down with him into the waters which make possible the one rebirth into immortality. Or, in the words of one of the antiphons sung by the Eastern Church on the Feast of the Epiphany: "When the forerunner saw him who is our Enlightenment, who enlightens every man, coming to be baptized, his heart rejoiced and his hand trembled. He pointed him out to the people and said: 'This is the Saviour of Israel who delivers us from corruption!'"[1]

The Eastern Church calls this feast "the Theophany," for it celebrates

---

[1]Most Rev. Joseph Raya and Baron Jose de Vinck, *Byzantine Daily Worship* (Allendale, N.J.: Alleluia Press, 1969), p. 592.

the appearance of God in human flesh. Here, the Byzantine liturgy says, is our Enlightenment, our perfect light. Here is the one light which is both wholly human and wholly divine. Here is the one light which is not reason only, but also love; not faith only, but also flesh; not hope only, but also experience; not only heaven opened, but earth reborn. Here is the one light which enlightens not merely the just and the bold and the holy, but the poor and the sinner as well. Here is the Enlightenment so splendid that it brings a silence deep enough for humankind to speak to God with God's own Word.

Our world lives in a darkness so vast, a forgetfulness so dreadful, that only a kind of global healing of memories can enlighten it. The healing of memories is in fact a healing of forgetfulness and the resurrection of memory. When the glory shining on the face of the risen Christ shines into our hearts, we are set free from the terrors that roam in the darkness, and the darkness itself flees away. Each moment of our lives is touched by the healing light of the Lord, and each becomes a moment in the history of salvation. The moment of rejection shines now with reconciliation; the moment of anger becomes bright with forgiveness; the moment of lust is filled with the radiance of love; and the countless moments of loneliness are radiant with the presence of him who will never leave us. Bitterness vanishes when we see the wounds others have inflicted upon us begin to gleam, like those of Christ, with the pure light of compassion. As he gazes upon all that we have tried to keep in darkness, his brightness touches too the wounds we have given others, not only the pain we have consciously caused, but the numberless hurts caused by our indifference, our coldness, our fear, our seemingly unbreakable absorption in our own poor selves. The human eyes of the Invisible Light fall on all of this, and we see the broken ones restored and raised up, and our shame itself is broken up, carried away into the darkness that lies behind the back of God.

When one's memory is healed, his or her life becomes very simply a mirror in which the mercy of the Father shining in the face of Christ is reflected. So too it will be for our world, when at last it discovers the source of the enlightenment it longs for even as it despairs of such a pure splendor. To see the earth reflect the face of God: that is what the Eastern Church sees on the feast of Enlightenment. As its priests bless all the waters of the earth, they sing:

> We glorify you, only-begotten Son, who have no father with your Mother, and no mother with your Father. In the feast just past we have seen you as a baby, and in this present feast we see you as a

> perfect man, O our perfect God, appearing out of perfection. For today we have attained the time of feasting, and the ranks of saints have joined us, and the angels celebrate together with men. Today the grace of the Holy Spirit in the likeness of a dove comes down upon the waters. Today there shines the Sun that never sets, and the world is sparkling with the light of the Lord. Today the moon is bright, together with the earth, in the glowing radiance of its light. Today the brilliant stars adorn the universe with the splendor of their shining. Today the clouds from heaven shed upon man a shower of justice. Today the Uncreated One willingly permits the hands of his creature to be laid upon him. Today the prophet and forerunner comes close to the Master, and he stands in awe, a witness of the condescension of God toward us. Today through the presence of the Lord the waters of the Jordan are changed into remedies. Today the whole universe is refreshed with mystical streams. . . . Today paradise has been opened to mankind, and the Sun of righteousness has shone upon us. . . . Today we escape from darkness and, through the light of the knowledge of God, we are illumined. Today the darkness of the world vanishes with the appearing of our God.[2]

As the Church sings of all created things praising the Holy Trinity who has made them and made them new by Christ's shining in the heart of humankind, it is looking forward to the day when its song will be sung by every man and woman ever born. Think of the light of the world, the promised one, the radiant Lord, standing with splendid face, not just in the presence of your pain or mine, but in the midst of every agony our race has experienced since the first sin. He is standing in Belfast, in Ethiopia, in Beirut, in Nicaragua, and in every village of Bangladesh. He is standing in Harlem and in northeast Brazil. He is standing in Auschwitz and Dachau and Buchenwald, at Wounded Knee and Babi Yar and Hiroshima. The sinless one is standing at Guadalcanal and Ypres, at Austerlitz and Moscow, at Gettysburg and at the Boyne, in the prisons of the Inquisition, at the broken walls of Constantinople, in the path of Genghis Khan. He is standing wherever men and women and children have suffered and wept and cursed and died since sin began. His face is shining on those who have no hope, and his pierced hands are touching those whose bodies are broken by disease, and his mercy is embracing all those imprisoned by loneliness or despair or sin. And everywhere he stands, glory pours from his face, touching all, blessing all, healing all.

---

[2]*Ibid.*, pp. 599–600.

"In my flesh I shall see God!" Job cried out, half in hope, half in despair. Every Job shall see God, and see him, as Job himself could not have dreamed to hope, in human flesh. God's human face looks on every human face, and when, at long last, each one singly and all of us together know and return that gaze, the whole human race will shine with uncreated light, wholly divine, wholly human.

"When you bowed your head to the forerunner, you crushed the heads of the dragons; and when you stood in the midst of the stream, you let your light shine upon all creatures that they might glorify you, our Savior, who enlighten our souls."[3] Even now, he is standing in the midst of the stream of our lives. His light shines upon us, and the beauty of his face shows us who we have become. And in the transfigured world, where heaven itself has found a home, the Spirit sings in us to the Father in praise of his love, which is our true enlightenment.

---

[3]*Ibid.*, p. 592.

THE GIFT THE MAGI RECEIVED

What made them set out, those magi?[1] What did they hope to find? What did the star tell them about the new-born king of the Jews? What did it promise them that they should have let it draw them forth from home to journey so many miles westward to search in (what was for them) such an unlikely place not for a wise man like themselves, but for a baby?

They were pagans, these magi, and they were astrologers, but they were also masters of all the elements. They knew the secrets of the earth and the air, of fire and water. They had waited patiently, in silence, for the earth to speak to them in the slow, careful syllables of herbs, in the many-voiced whisperings of leaves, in the languages of bears and rabbits. They had learned the grammar of acorns and could prophesy the shape of oaks. Their words had been molded by the silent shapes of desert hills.

They had listened day after day to the air. They had yielded to the wind that they might discover whence it comes and where it goes. They had sung with the nightingale and flown with the falcon, and trembling, they had felt the shadow of the griffin's wings. They could read the book the sun writes every day, and even in their sleep they could do the sums of the moon.

They knew the voices of rivers and had explored the caverns of the sea. They had let the tides carry them out into nameless currents where all their bones were melted and they became as fluid as the waves. When they returned, they knew the mysteries of the blood, and could trace the liquid patterns of the human spirit.

Fire had burned their hearts. It had left them empty and so still that their eyes looked always to the marrows of things. It had given them

---

[1]The sense of what the magi must have been like was given to me by Ursula Le Guin in her book *A Wizard of Earthsea* (New York: Parnassus Press, 1968).

true ears to hear those things speak their real names. The words they spoke fell like sparks on the world.

The magi knew the language of the stars, of course. The planets told them stories in simple declarative sentences—bluff, bold Jupiter and dazzling Venus and elusive Mercury. Beyond them the stars sang in the desert nights, faintly, with steadier, stranger voices. In their yearly ebb and flow they wove a subtle incantation—not a spell of luck and chance as the ignorant then and now believe, not the chain of cause and consequence that the half-wise seek to forge, but a simple insistent word that the magi had come to know testified to the way each of the eternal spheres was fixed unalterably in its endlessly turning course.

Not that the word of the stars made the magi despair: no, they understood too well how, within the perfect balance that all things kept, patterns here and there could be reshaped, this figure or that could be transformed, moments now and again could be speeded, slowed, or ever so delicately shifted into some new phase. The magi were content to spend their years learning the true names of things and drawing into their burned hearts the threads of all the vast powers of the universe—the forces of light, the energies of gravity and mass, the immense dynamism of dissolution itself—so that when summoned, when the time was right and an opening showed itself, they might speak the right word in the right language and bring a blessing to an old woman or a goat or a king.

No, the magi did not despair. Their wisdom had taught them humility, and the humble do not despair. But at times they did grow sad. It is not easy to describe their sadness. It was not exactly suffering that made them sad, though it was never easy for them to acknowledge how few were the creatures, human or animal or otherwise, they were able to pluck from the net of pain. It was not death that saddened them, though often they used their healing skills on their own hearts as they stood on the far boundaries of life and watched as children, kind rulers, young mothers fled before them through the twilight into the country of the dead. Nor was it boredom that made them sad, the inner fatigue that feeds on a surfeit of knowledge, where the whole univese is stripped of flesh and its dry bones crammed into the maw of an already gorged brain. No: even if the light that shone within them had changed for them the ghosts and gods their countrymen sensed everywhere into more familiar shapes, the magi knew that this very familiarity sprang from such an intermeshing of names and powers, persisted with such marvelous solidity in the face of the darkness that flickered all about it, that they never grew tired of seeing how even the smallest thing spoke not only its own name, but the name of all the rest.

It was just here, somehow, that their occasional sadness took root – in their evergrowing awareness that the name of all the rest, the word that encompassed all their words, was a nameless name, unuttered and unutterable, unknown and unknowable, forever hinted at, forever silent. The magi were lords of language, and kings came to them barefooted, bearing rich gifts, to learn the words that would lift a drought or stop a war or heal a city. They were the masters of the secrets of the heart, and even though they lived in solitude, each had others, two or three, as many as most men ever have, who knew his own true name. Even love was not a stranger to them. Yet the magi knew that a nameless ignorance clouded their deepest souls, and the souls of every man and woman who had ever lived, so that some insatiable hunger gnawed them in secret and kept them from whatever knowledge, whatever act it was that would give them the perfect joy that forever eluded them.

So it happened, I think that when they saw the star that spoke to them of the newborn King of Jews they were not reluctant to set out on their difficult journey. The star made no promises. It summoned them. They were used to that. Even the song of an unknown bird is a summons to a wise man. The star simply told them to go and give homage to the new-born King, and they obeyed.

I do not know the word that the unexpected radiance of this star gave to them. I think that it did not speak to them in Persian or in any of the other ancient languages they normally used to say the real names of things. I suspect that when the star told the magi to give homage, it spoke in Hebrew and used the Hebrew word for "fall prostrate before." Certainly that would not have surprised the magi; they knew what to do in the presence of kings, even infant kings. Yet there was something strange in this word, some odd shape that caught in their mouths when they said it, some odd feeling that caught in their hearts when they remembered it, something elusive and nameless that, even if it did not make any promises or stir any hopes, rang in the ignorance of their deepest souls and drew them across all those wintry desert miles to the city of the Jewish kings.

As the magi neared Jerusalem, their silence deepened. They were used to silence. They were lords of language, but because they were servants of light, not darkness, they had long since learned that light breathes its words only into the clear spaces of silence. But the silence that enfolded them now was so huge that it almost frightened them. The star grew brighter, and its word more urgent, and the enormous silence in them pulled that word down into them, down into the cloud of nameless ignorance that lay still in their deepest souls.

The magi knew Herod at once for what he was. They did not have to trick him or cast a spell on him or weave a net of illusion about him. They played him as a wise angler might play a wily old bass so accustomed to lures that it has forgotten what a worm looks like. They stood there in their strange clothes, their faces calm, speaking the simple truth in their odd accents, and Herod bit. He found out what they needed to know, told them, then lied to them, and sent them on their way, so caught up in schemes and so sure that they were not what they seemed that it never occurred to him that they would know that he was exactly what he seemed. As for his evil plans, they trusted somehow that the true King would bring life where Herod meant to sow death.

And so the magi moved through the night toward Bethlehem. Now the star went before them, no longer summoning, but guiding them, its radiance so filling them that all the names they knew fell away from them into the silence that wholly possessed them. They were empty now, bearing within themselves only that nameless cloud that no longer seemed like ignorance, but shone with the brightness of the word the star had given them.

Then they were at the door of the stable, their hearts beating against their ribs, their fingers stiff around the precious gifts their hands still carried. They pushed open the door, and stepped in. They could smell the cows and hear them gently chewing their cuds. A few sheep looked up at them with quiet eyes. In a corner, on a clean blanket laid over the straw, sat a young woman, a girl really, with a baby on her lap. Her husband stood by her side, and the baby played with his mother's fingers. She looked at the magi, and was still.

They came a few steps closer, then stopped. Their gifts hung at their sides, useless. They had nothing to give. Their words had all dropped away, vanished into the namelessness that was revealing itself in them. They knew nothing—no languages, no secrets, no mysteries. Earth and air, water and fire were silent. The stars were dumb, and the measureless powers of the universe itself were wordless in the magis' hearts. Even the abrupt syllables of pain and death were hushed, and sadness too had disappeared. The wise men stood there, still, voiceless, lost in wonder before the girl and her baby, no longer even knowing what they did not know.

Then the girl picked up the baby and set him on her lap. She smiled at the magi, and said, "His name is Jesus." They looked him in the face as she spoke his name, and saw, as another wise man saw, that his eyes were the color of glory. Then, suddenly but very gently, they felt that glory reach into their deepest souls to embrace the silent radiance now shining there. And as it did, they felt that cloud of namelessness break open and receive its true name, the name that the mother had named her Son. Then the magi knew that it was to him that all their words belonged, and as those words returned, still and lovely in the glory that filled them, they offered them to him, one upon another, some as rich as gold, some as fragrant as incense, some as deep as myrrh.

And the words became a song in the wise men's hearts, the song the universe is always singing, and as the universe sang that song in them, sang it to the one whose name sings the universe itself into life, the magi knew that beyond all songs, beyond knowledge, beyond wisdom, beyond silence, beyond even love, they were receiving from this new-born King the word that the star had spoken in them. As he spoke it in them, their whole being leaped to greet it, and they found they knew it, had always known it. The word was worship, and when their hearts spoke it, they found that they could say the baby's name, and they said it, and then, falling down on their faces in the dry, sweet straw, they adored him.

THE FEAST OF MEETING

The Byzantine liturgy calls the feast of the Presentation of Christ in the Temple on February 2, *hypapante* or, in English, "meeting."

On Christmas God reveals his human face, and shepherds come to look at him in wonder. At Epiphany the eternal light of God shining now in human flesh fills the whole earth, and draws the first Gentiles to worship him.

But on the feast of meeting the Son of God goes forth to meet his people for the first time. In eternity he rides on the songs of the angels, and throughout the cosmos he walks on the wings of the galactic winds, but on earth and in time he is carried by his Mother. He has made her a cloud of light so that as his glory is translated into human form not the least ray of it is dimmed. The heart, an ancient Chinese poem says, is an endless river of stars, and this immaculate image of the heart, this Jewish girl, is lovelier and more splendid than the Milky Way in summer. She brings her royal Son to meet his people, and his first gift to her is not a crown, but a sword.

It is evening. As the winter light leaks away, the clouds that have hidden the sun all day hurry to the east, leaving the sky smooth and still. In the southwest, above the maple bush on the hill, Venus appears. Soon it will be night, and in the growing darkness my mind is peering toward Jerusalem. It is as if the radiant images of faith are great luminous torches, driving back the shadows, revealing the mystery embedded in every human presence.

Joseph and Mary bring Jesus to the Temple, and Simeon and Anna meet the Messiah. With their own eyes they see the consolation of Israel in the flesh of a baby. In some dim corner of this Temple that piled and arched around them they hold in their old hands a tiny, living body and receive in their hearts the knowledge that the one they have waited all these years to see has come to meet them at last.

I have been wondering all day long if I ever met a man like Simeon. I have known many women like Anna, or so they seem to me: old women who spend all their time in church, whose faded eyes and worn-out ears can see and hear things that most others cannot. I remember one especially, and I can see her still, after thirty years, bent, dressed always in black, scurrying down the street under the full summer trees. Her eyes were fastened on some other place, and she went toward it with such intensity that she seemed to tear great holes in the air as she passed. I was ten or twelve, yet she was smaller than I was, and she smelled strange, like unopened rooms and foreign food. Her passion scared me a little, and I thought maybe she was crazy. Maybe she was, but maybe that is not what I really thought because after so many years I remember her still, because now I see the bond between us, because I too have learned to hurry crazily to the same place she went to.

And suddenly I realize that I *have* known a man like Simeon. He lived in the Hope Mission in the city where I went to college. The mission reached out to the needy with kindness, but not perhaps with much hope. Some students used to go there to help out, and sometimes we played checkers or rummy with the old pensioners who lived there. They were all Catholics, and we were all Protestants, and we used to discuss among ourselves ways of drawing them out of their rooms for a little companionship.

Most of them were happy to accommodate us, but one old man was adamant. He had no time, he said. He needed to spend all of the little time he had left in prayer, preparing himself to meet God. How that perplexed us! In those days we didn't speak of building community, but our American instincts were repelled all the same by such solitariness, by such single-minded devotion. Perhaps we even called it fanaticism or fear. Still, the thought of that old man bent over his prayer-book haunted me. I was fascinated by the totality of his fascination, by the passionate activity of his waiting.

Since then I have learned a little about the human shapes of waiting: the father's body leaning forward as he looks each day down the road on which his prodigal son sped away from him; the tilt of a mother's head as she listens even in sleep for her child's cry; the openness of eyes searching crowds at airports or bus depots for friends or lovers; the curve of stillness that shapes a woman's whole being as she waits for the sight of that face whose image already fills her heart. And I have learned a little about the way that the deepest souls of all of us, men or women, assume the shape of that same curve as we yearn in prayer to meet and encompass the one who, when he comes at last, will encompass us.

But what does it mean, finally, to speak of waiting for and then meeting the One who is always present, whose beauty and love fill all things? What did those days and hours mean when we curved toward the hearts of others, and beyond them to the stars, and beyond even them to God? What were those weeks about when our whole bodies ached like rotten teeth, and what was the meaning of those interminable nights when we wept and tossed and slept and woke again to weep, longing for a presence that was never really absent? And what of those years, that time of waste and sad distraction, when our waiting was so intense that we could not wait at all? Was it all a mistake, a misunderstanding? Did we need a better psychology, a more intelligent theology, finer training in prayer? Were we simply too impatient to be mystics, perhaps?

But there is another way of looking at our waiting, a way that this feast of meeting gives us. What were Simeon and Anna waiting for? God? But they knew God, or they would not have spent all their time in his temple. Mystical experience? The Holy Spirit had spoken to Simeon, and Anna was a prophetess. They had had more mystical experience than most mystics. The Messiah, the salvation of Israel and the redemption of Jerusalem? Yes, but what does that mean? This, I think: "The Lord whom you seek will suddenly come to his temple" (Mal 3:1).

They believed in the promise and wanted to see with their own eyes God's refining fire. They sought what Moses could not see on the mountain. They sought the vision that later made the face of Moses so radiant that no one could gaze on it. They were waiting for God's eyes to look on the world, not from above, but in the world, so that as he saw it, it might become again what it had been in the beginning when he first saw all that he had made: very good.

The Byzantine liturgy says that when Simeon saw the human face of God and felt on his own face the everlasting light pouring from God's human eyes, he wanted to run to tell Adam the Good News of the Incarnation—that at last all was well again, that his children would never need to hide again. But Simeon did not know everything. He could not yet have understood that in the tiny, living body he held cupped in his hands the fullness of God lived as that fullness does not live even in the whole immensity of the universe. Neither he nor Anna could have known fully, though they guessed it a bit, how before too long that same body would be rent asunder and in three days transformed so that all human bodies might become the dwelling-places of the very Presence hidden behind the veil in the Holy of Holies.

Nor could they have known fully how the "light of revelation" pouring from God's human eyes in God's human face would transform every human face and give to all human eyes the vision of God's eyes. They had waited to see the glory of God's face, and that glory had come, and soon its radiance would shine on every human face.

That is the radiance we have ached to see. That is the glory of love we have longed to meet. That is what the feast of meeting promises and proclaims. The father bending toward his lost son, the mother yearning toward her child, friends and lovers and all of us at prayer curving through eyes and hearts toward the beloved – all the human curves of waiting are met, embraced, and become a circle of endless joy as the curve of God's own yearning takes flesh in Jesus and comes to meet us.

Blind and foolish, we have so often ravaged those human hearts we loved as we tried to seize in them the infinite love we longed for. Ashamed, we have wept because we have hurt them and forgotten God. But God, all tenderness and joy, has held out to us a child and has asked us to let his glory fall upon our faces and his love make its home in our hearts. If we do, if we come to meet him who has come to meet us, we will see the radiance on his face, and our waiting will be transformed. We will see his radiance on the face of every face we have loved, on the face of every face we meet, and their joy when they meet us will tell us that on our faces too shines the glory of the Only-begotten of the Father, in whom he is well pleased.

2 THE COMING OF FIRE

INTO THE NEW CREATION

February: icebox month, month of the deep freeze, heart of winter, month of Ash Wednesday. Fly south; drug yourself with Carnival, light a candle for the arrogant Caesars, Julius and Augustus, who each stole a day from it to add to the summer luster of the months they gave their names to; daily count the minutes of the sun's increase, and nightly feast on Orion's magnificence; ski, skate, and sled: February still is a cold passage between Christmas and Easter, an icy limbo where we wait for the unlocked waters, the kind intimation of spring.

Still, each February begins with the Feast of Meeting, the encounter in the Temple with Mary and the Child – not Groundhog Day, but Candlemas, a feast of light when, dark or bright, the glory of Israel and the joy of the Gentiles shows himself, hidden and shadowless, in the center of the temple not made with human hands. And listen to T. S. Eliot:

> Midwinter spring is its own season
> Semipiternal though sodden towards sundown,
> Suspended in time, between pole and tropic.
> When the short day is brightest, with frost and fire,
> The brief sun flames the ice, on pond and ditches,
> In windless cold that is the heart's heat,
> Reflecting in a watery mirror
> A glare that is blindness in the early afternoon.
> And glow more intense than blaze of branch, or brazier,
> Stirs the dumb spirit: no wind, but pentecostal fire
> In the dark time of the year. Between melting and freezing
> The soul's sap quivers.[1]

Once, as I walked near our farm on a midwinter's day very much

[1]"Little Gidding," *Four Quartets*, p.138.

like the one Eliot writes of, I began to hear beneath the squeaking of my boots on the dry snow a strange sound. I stopped to listen to it more carefully. Nothing moved. No chainsaws whined, no snowmobiles roared, no cars broke the quiet, not even from a distance. All human voices were hushed, and the earth too was still. No wind blew, no dog barked, no crow or jay called, no branch creaked, no icicle dripped. I stood and listened to the sound of silence. It filled my mind, my body. I could almost hear my heart beat. In the solitude of that vast stillness, if I had had words, I would have wondered, as Eliot once had, "Where is the summer, the unimaginable/Zero summer?"[2]

Zero summer? Yes, and light invisible, bright sadness, crucified life, God in the flesh; the pentecostal fire blazes in the icy limbo because the changeless one has immersed himself in the river of our becoming. Life has drained the cup of death and has filled it with his blood. In Jesus Christ, all contradictions are contradicted and united.

Is it any wonder the straight path twists our being tighter than a pig's tail? Call it what you will—paradox, irony, koan, or simply mystery—the Gospel life feels strange, oddly like death, because it stands life as we know it on its head. Jesus says, "Happy are you who are poor: yours is the kingdom of God. Happy you who are hungry now: you shall be satisfied. Happy you who weep now: you shall laugh. Happy are you when people hate you, drive you out, abuse you, denounce your name as criminal, on account of the Son of Man. Rejoice when that day comes and dance for joy, for then your reward will be great in heaven" (Luke 6:20-23). Feels like death? Prize poverty, hunger, tears, and contempt, despise riches, fullness, laughter, and praise—and then dance? That is not just death. That is a funeral celebration—except that in this case our feet are beating time on the roof of an empty tomb.

The Romans called us enemies of the human race, and the Marxists think we are purveyors of alienation, but God's foolishness is wiser than the wisdom of men. The Eastern Church has a word for what God is up to in his Son: *theosis.* All those odd parables, strange reversals, bizarre contradictions, and especially the final, and most baffling somersault of all—the cross, Life put to death—have the single purpose of trampling on death by death and lavishing life on an entire cosmos that lay, mostly without knowing it, in a tomb of its

---

[2]Ibid.

own making. But not just any life. *Theosis* means divinization, deification. "He who descended is the very one who ascended higher than all the heavens that he might fill all things" (Eph 4:10). Through the glorified flesh of his crucified and risen Son the Father pours his light, his fire, his very glory into all of creation to make it what he meant it to be from the beginning – his true image and likeness, in a manner beyond understanding the sharer of his own divine being.

True, we groan with all creation as we await the final resurrection of our bodies (Rom 8:22-23), but already we are a new creation. Already Christ is risen, and we have died and risen with him. By the pouring of the baptismal waters and the outpouring of the baptizing Spirit we have been immersed in his life. Already we are "a new creation; the old has gone, the new has come" (2 Cor 5:17). Our new life is not waiting for us out there in the future or up there in heaven. Already our feet are standing in the courts of the New Jerusalem, our faces bathed in the radiance of the unimaginable zero summer. Already the anointing of the Spirit runs from the tops of our heads to the tips of our toes. Already the unencompassable God is our Abba. Already our almighty Lord Jesus has come in and feasts with us in the center of our hearts.

This is why we celebrate the saints, especially the Mother of God. They show us that the victory of the Lord Jesus has already taken place in human flesh. And this is what faith means: in the darkness of the world, against the lies of Satan, in the twisting of our own being as it is hauled into glory – to hold fast to the victory of Jesus. This alone is absolutely real. Pain bites, loss grieves, fear grips, sin clings, death looms, but the only absolute reality is the risen Lord Jesus Christ and the Kingdom that he has revealed in our midst and placed in our hearts.

But then Lent chills us like February's ice. Bad enough to be burdened still with February; why afflict ourselves with Lent? For those who have made friends with tears and waltz the night away with loss Lent is already a midwinter spring. But for the rest of us it unlocks the healing waters of Jesus's words: "Not everyone who says to me, 'Lord, Lord,' will enter the kingdom of heaven, but only he who does the will of my father in heaven" (Matt 7:21). Or as St. Paul might have said, "New creation is as new creation does." Simple: the more we live the risen life – the life of love, of compassion, of childlikeness, of praise – the more we experience resurrection. The more we live as new creatures, the more we are a new creation.

But not simple: the more we live and even feel like a new creation, the more the unimaginable zero summer seems simply unimaginable zero. "Last Tuesday I saw the light, and now my heart is a black hole." "I experienced the release of the Spirit last year, and now I am a worse sinner than before." "Ever since I joined Madonna House, my skin feels as if it is being stripped from my body." It may take longer than a few weeks or months, and the pain may be largely illusion or neurosis or temptation, but still, all this is normal. When we start to live in the truth of the glorious victory of the Lord Jesus, suddenly we see and feel the power of death in us, around us, for the first time. Only when the light shines in the darkness is the darkness revealed for what it is. Only when life seizes us can we smell the embrace of death as it, literally, tries to squeeze the life out of us.

Then we are tempted to a great sadness; faced with the enormous gap between where we have been and where we are going, not able to believe in the glory that the Lord has given us, we reach out and try to pick up our old life. At that moment, we find ourselves dancing with a corpse. Baffled by the dance of life, we dance instead with a putrid corpse.

God is good. He made us for the riches of his love, the laughter of his joy, the fullness of his life, the praise of his glory, not for tears and poverty, emptiness and contempt. God is good. He loved us so much that when we were dead, he sent his Son, like Elijah in Zarephath, to embrace our death and raise us to new life. God is so good that he has poured his Spirit upon all flesh to claim every tear, every pain, every loneliness, every ugliness for his dance of love, every work of human sin for the work of his mercy.

Can you hear the words of our good Lord, Jesus? "Come, dance with me. Let me share with you the joy of my victorious cross. Let me give you laughter in tears, life in death, light in darkness, summer in winter. Already I am everything and am in everything. Already you are in me and I am in you. Come: in all the places where there is death in you I will dance the dance of life with you. Let my love cast out your fear. How? Don't I know my name? Won't I come when you call me? Won't I be Jesus for you when you ask? Come to those places where you are not a new creation, and I will be the new creation in you. Come to my cross, and I will be your Master."

We fear Lent because it is the time of the cross, but can you see in the blaze of sun or snow, in the sky-blue shadows along the ground, how the cross of Jesus is light, not darkness? By forgetting what we already are, we make Lent into an image of our old, ungraced selves and end up dancing, gracelessly, with our own corpses. If instead we let go of our endless striving to keep body and soul together, and let ourselves fall into the freely given light within us, our Lent will shine with that Easter sun that has already risen in our hearts.

Pray: let the Father speak the words of his love in you. Fast: let your emptiness show you the face of Jesus filling you with light. Give alms: let the radiance of your brother and your sister reveal to you your own glory. Dance: step across the threshold of sadness into the new creation, that midwinter spring of repentance that already blooms, beyond taste or smell or sight, in February's bright flowers of pentecostal ice.

REPENT AND BELIEVE

What made Zaccheus do it? We don't quite know. We only know the bare facts: that Zaccheus, "a chief tax collector, and rich," wanted to see Jesus so badly that when the crowd blocked his view, he climbed a tree to make sure that he saw him (see Lk 19:1-10). Small-town crook,[1] pipsqueak big-shot though he was, probably even forgetting to spit out the half-smoked cigar that always stuck out of the corner of his mouth, he forgot too about the sneers of the local gentry and clambered up a sycamore to gape at this wonder-working preacher from up north who just happened to be passing through town.

We don't know, exactly, what made him do it. We would like to think that all sinners have hearts of gold, but it isn't so. After all, do you? Do I? No, not all prostitutes are sweeter and more honest than married ladies and innocent virgins. Not all gangsters are misunderstood little boys aching for Holy Communion, and corrupt politicans feasting on the blood of the poor are not really doing the best they can in a tough world. We would like to think so, because then we would be let off the hook, but when that other tax-collector was moaning for mercy and beating his breast in the back of the church, he meant it and he needed it.

No, if prostitutes and gangsters are going into the kingdom of heaven ahead of the rest of us, it is not because they are, at bottom, better than we are. Nor is it that they are worse. But something in Zaccheus made him discontent with his crooked life, something that has made him for twenty centuries, and will make him forever, a symbol of every sinner who wants a new life, something beyond a natural big-heartedness or an innate childlikeness. He was in touch with a yearning within him that he could not satisfy and that could not be

[1]Father Francis Martin first suggested this image of Zaccheus to me.

satisfied except—by what? He didn't know. He only knew that he wanted to see Jesus, wanted to know what kind of man he was.

And what kind of man did he turn out to be, this Jesus? He was a man who "came to seek and save the lost" (Lk 19:10). He was a man who took away sin and gave new life. He was, and is the Savior, and will be until sin is gone forever and only the glory of his life in all creatures remains.

Sin is a terrible burden, the weight of the whole world's evil pulling our hearts into a darkness worse than annihilation. It begins so simply with little acts of rejection or mere non-acceptance that hook into our infantile need for total love and create in us fear and rage, guilt and sadness. By the time we reach adulthood, even if we have been baptized as babies and raised as Christians, almost all of us have chosen again and again and again to be accomplices in our own rejection. We choose to be woven into the web of selfish fear that is the world's darkness. We choose to believe in the absence of God, and that absence weighs on our hearts with such constant force that we think it is as normal as gravity.

Then one day, who knows when, we hear that Jesus is passing by. Perhaps we have heard it every Sunday of our lives, but this day that weight of God's absence in us at last wearies us beyond pride, beyond fear, breaks through to that core of us where we are all emptiness, all longing, and we want only to know one thing; what kind of man is this Jesus? Suddenly, without knowing how we got there, we are up in that tree with Zaccheus, our whole being in our eyes, looking for the face of Jesus. And Jesus looks at us and says, "Hurry up and come down! I *must* stay at your house today." (Lk 19:5).

All that waiting, those dreadful years, and it turns out that God has been waiting for us. His absence vanishes in the clear human eyes of Jesus—and with it go all our sins. When Zaccheus let Jesus look at him and speak to him and invite himself to his house, he was free, reborn really. That whole complex life he had built—the lies, the cheating, the betrayal of his people, the fawning over Romans, the turning from God, the spitting on the Torah, the squalid love-affair with his own emptiness—all of it was gone except the money he had made from it. And he ran all the way home to get rid of that too in a blast of generosity as unconditioned as the generosity God had shown him in Jesus.

Do you think Zaccheus gave a nice party for the Lord? The kind where everyone sits around and drinks tea, or maybe sherry, and talks about God and the finer points of theology? Do you think Zaccheus got refined as well as reborn? I doubt it. The tables were loaded with food and with all the wine his toadies and gofers could find. The place was in a uproar. People were dancing and shouting, and in the corners slick operators with worried looks on their faces were trying to figure out what their next move was now that old Zaccheus had apparently got religion. The poor were crowding around all the doors and windows, appearing as if by magic as the news spread, dogs were barking, cats yowling, donkeys three blocks away braying their heads off. The neighbors would have called the cops, but the cops were already there, their spears stacked in the hallway, stuffing themselves with lamb and wine, ogling the pretty ladies along with everyone else.

And Jesus? Well, I suppose he was enjoying himself too. The party was his idea, after all. When the time came for him to reply to Zaccheus' renunciation of his money, Jesus recognized him as one of his own. And then he told a story, evidently, about God's preference for those who are willing to go out on a limb for him. . . . Yes, I think Jesus enjoyed the party.

Do we? Lent comes, Jesus comes striding out of the desert, asking us to "repent and believe the good news," and are we running to see his face and to join the Easter party? More probably we are slinking away in some other direction, if only from our fear that Jesus comes to add to our burden rather than to take it away. What a blasphemy—and who of us is altogether free of it?

"Repent" means to turn around, to stop believing in the absence of God, to stop building a life without him, to stop trying to find rest by our own efforts—and, like Zaccheus, to start climbing the tree of salvation so that we can see the life-creating face of Jesus. Each year the Lord in his Church calls us to turn from anything in us that denies his victory on the cross so that our whole being may lay hold of the risen life *already* in us through the out-pouring of the Holy Spirit in baptism and in all those thousands of "baptismal" moments when we let Jesus look at us and become truly Jesus for us. It is not some roving Galilean or preacher, known by hearsay, whom our hearts are calling us to run toward. It is the Messiah, the Lord of glory, the crucified and risen Son of God, whose name the Holy Spirit has written on our own spirits, who wants to know if we'd like to come to the party he is already celebrating in us.

It is a serious business all right, but serious does not mean gloomy. I imagine that Zaccheus, cigar clenched between his teeth, robe tucked up to show his skinny legs, for all his eagerness knew that if what he hoped could possibly be true, he would shortly be inconveniencing himself even more thoroughly than that scratchy sycamore was as he climbed it. But like Abraham, whose prodigal son he was, and like Moses, whose disobedient pupil he had been, he knew that the face he hoped to see was so filled with light that it would cast out gloom forever.

"The hour is coming, and is here *now,* when the dead will hear the voice of the Son of God, and those who hear will live" (Jn 5:25). If we let him, Jesus will show us the fullness of his Father's love. If we want, we can tune our ears to the inner noise of our longing and come to hear it for what it really is: the Lord's knocking at the door of our hearts. If we take the risk of faith, God will show us in the radiant face of his Son that he has become God-with-us, that he has put to death our death and lavished on us immortal life. If we let him, he will feast with us, not merely for an evening, but always, and we will at least begin to taste our Easter even on Ash Wednesday.

ON SEEING THE FACE OF CHRIST

These days I am meditating on "seeing." Lent is here, and I am conscious nearly always that we are called to see the face of Christ. Light of Light, God of God, has taken our flesh for his own. The God of all the galaxies, the immortal Light beyond all light, has slept in his Mother's arms. He has been baptized in the Jordan River, and he has transformed not just the water made into wine at Cana, but the whole earth. All things were made through him, and he has touched them with our flesh so that now they reveal his glory, the glory of the Only-begotten of the Father. In his death he went into the deepest heart of creation – its emptiness – and when he rose, he took our flesh and filled it with the glory of God. The face of Christ is shining now in every human face, and that is why these days I am meditating on "seeing."

Staretz Silouan, the great Russian monk of Mount Athos, saw the living Christ standing by the holy doors of his monastery church. He felt on his heart, as his biographer says, "the gentle gaze of the joyous, all-forgiving, boundlessly-loving Christ,"[1] and was filled with the Holy Spirit, and his soul was opened to the light of heaven. Yet for many years afterward, once the vision had faded, he suffered dreadfully as he learned to embrace even the enemies of God in his love of Christ. How, then, do we come to see the face of Christ and to experience his joyous, life-giving gaze on our hearts? How can we see and never forget? How can we see, and then long to see more?

When I spent the summer of 1959 at Marian Centre in Edmonton, I saw the face of the crucified Christ in the men we served there. I did not see his face in the same way that Staretz Silouan saw it, but in faith I knew that the struggle and the loneliness of the men was the pain of Christ. He taught us that he was one with the hungry, the

[1]Archimandrite Sophrony, *The Monk of Mount Athos: Staretz Silouan 1866-1938*, trans. Rosemary Edmonds (Oxford: Mowbrays, 1973), p.19.

thirsty, the homeless (Matt 25:31ff). He told us that we could never see his Father if we did not let faith teach us a new way of seeing our brothers and sisters, and he showed me a little of his suffering in the faces of those whom the world rejected as it had rejected him.

But years later, during another visit to Marian Centre, I saw in the men the radiant face of Christ risen and glorious. They are still suffering, but I saw in them a calmness, a wholeness, a beauty, a light that I had not seen fifteen years before. A new friend of the Centre told me how moved he was to see the staff treat the men "like princes." Yes, I thought, princes, that's what they are, the sons of a King. They had not changed. My eyes had changed. What changed my eyes? What light made me see before the Christ who needed comfort and now the Christ who comforted me?

There are answers to these questions, answers that come from the mind. There is a time for such answers, but only when the mind is resting in the heart, where it too can look on the compassionate face of Christ. There are other answers, simpler answers, heart-answers, and these are the answers that interest me now. What changed the yes of Staretz Silouan and is changing my eyes too into heart-eyes, Gospel-eyes, God-eyes? Love. Who changed them? It is Love who changed them – God our merciful Father breathing forth the Spirit in his risen Son, Jesus Christ, secretly touching them, and saying, "Let there be light."

I am meditating on "seeing," and I see that love creates sight. I see too that God, the Holy Trinity, who is Love, breathes our sight into life through the love of others. For fifteen years, as I studied and was ordained and studied, as I tried to walk with Christ, my brothers and sisters at Marian Centre were trying to walk with him too. His way is love, and on bright days and dark, month after month, year after year, seeing or not seeing, they loved the image of Christ in the men into brightness. They made the stew and served it and washed the floor and listened and prayed and cared for those whom the Father sent them with as much reverence and patience as they could summon. They must have wept blood sometimes too, and begged for light for their own blindness. And their tears, their longing, their love, began to make the image of Christ, in their own hearts as well as in the hearts of the men, glow with the deep luster of an old icon restored to its original beauty.

But during all those years so many other brothers and sisters were restoring the icon of my heart too. I find that work of restoration too vast for my imagination. The care of those who have loved me, their generosity and their tears and above all their prayers – such care, as I consider it, seems to move from the hundreds of small acts of love that I remember into a single, cosmic work of mercy more intricate and more splendid than the whole universe. What do I know of how the immensity of God was focused on the smallness of me through the love of others, who in turn were fed and healed and given sight by others, in their turn loved by still others until the whole network of humankind is implicated?

What I do know is that it was so. What I begin to see is that all "seeing" is of a piece, woven out of many threads, each of which is spun by love. "Seeing" is single because love is finally single, because love in all its human variety is finally the image of Love. My seeing depends upon the interwoven energies of the whole race, and the passion of God himself in Jesus Christ, because when I finally see, I will see the face of Christ shining on every human face. God squanders all his love simply to make me see because when at last I see Christ, God becomes true God for me. God involves all men and women in my "seeing" because, when my eye is single, I will see a single Christ looking on me with love from the face of each man and each woman, and each will become the image of Love that he or she truly is.

Love creates sight. Love opened the eyes of Staretz Silouan after years of anguish to the gaze of Christ, not just in the Church of St. Elias, but in every human heart. Love has made the faces of the men who pass through Marian Centre bright with the glory of Christ. Love too has given me whatever sight I have or will ever have. I have learned a little to see the sons and daughters of the King, mostly because others have looked on me with love, but also because I knew, through the gospel within me, that the only thing that mattered for me was to look on others with love. For me, as for them, there was the discipline of prayer and work, the discipline of suffering, joy, and love, as I struggled to see what the Lord himself promised me was there to be seen when I first knew that his love had looked me into life. And so, as I looked on my brothers and sisters, on my friends, on my blood family, on those for whom I am a father in Christ, on anyone the Father sent into my heart, I knew more clearly each year what it was like to be looked on by Christ. As I touched the tenderness that I newly discovered within me, I discovered also the tenderness of Christ for me and understood that by love is Love revealed.

Love reveals the face of Christ. When I meditate on this, I reflect most deeply on his Mother. All the saints are his radiant images, and the images of those images can become windows into his everlasting light. Yet his Mother was so pure that when the Father looked upon her, she received from him all of that light and gave that light in return her own flesh. Slowly, I came to know the touch of her eyes on me, and in her love found the courage to go into the depths of others' hearts, and my own, to seek the face of her Son, who promised to be there for me.

It is Lent, and I am meditating on "seeing." I knew that Lent meant "spring," but just today I learned that the word was derived from an old word meaning "to lengthen." In spring the days lengthen and the sun grows brighter, warmer. Light, reborn at the winter solstice, begins to fill the whole world with radiance. Lent has seemed a grim time, a sad time, but its discipline of faith and truth brings instead a time of growing light. The Church calls us to stand in truth, to look, to become as attentive as lovers, and so to see in the clear light of faith the face of our Beloved.

See how quietly he is standing there where we thought nothing was. The brightness of his Easter face touches all that is most hidden in us. His compassionate and boundlessly-loving eyes rest on our deepest hearts, and they are no longer frozen. We sense the great river of the Spirit flowing in us, and we hear that river singing, "Come to the Father." He who "first commanded light to shine out of darkness" has flooded our hearts with light. Our unveiled faces gaze upon "the glory of the Lord as we are being transformed from glory to glory into his very image" (2 Col 3:18). God said, "Let there be light." And there is light. It shines on the glorious face of Love made visible and fills all creation, and especially our own healing hearts, with beauty.

WITH CHRIST IN THE DESERT

After God had publicly claimed Jesus as his beloved Son, Jesus began his ministry. He began it not in the excitement of miracles or with the sounds of words, but in the solitude and the silence of the desert. After John had baptized him and the Father had acknowledged him, "the spirit immediately drove him out into the wilderness. And he was in the wilderness forty days, tempted by Satan; and he was with the wild beasts, and the angels ministered to him" (Mk 1:12-13).

Every Lent the Spirit urges the Church to spend forty days with Christ in the desert. This is a time of recognition and quiet intimacy. It is a time to fast from food so that we can also fast from falsehood. The Spirit does not call us to project ourselves into the physical world of Jesus, to bewail our sins as if we had no remedy for them, to thrust our minds into the tangled roots of our own lives. Instead, he calls us to stop running from Jesus, to turn around and look with his eyes at the empty places stretching through us and all around us where we have denied Jesus access, and to let the Lord enter those places. Where he enters, God's love enters, and where God's love is, there is Easter.

Easter: how we long to get there, to live there always, but we cannot until the Father speaks, until the Spirit drives us to open our eyes to the wastes of isolation within us, without us, and Christ comes to make those wastes bloom with his love. There are many kinds of desert—empty quarters of the heart where the failure to receive and to give love has stifled life and growth; wildernesses of the world's marketplaces where everything is exchanged except love; dark spaces like oceans of stone lying between those whose union God means to show forth his own Triune joy. Into all these Christ has come. If we let ourselves believe and choose his presence in our darknesses, he will enable us to see him, to *know* him in faith. Then where there has been nothing, and worse than nothing, Easter will happen at last.

Of course there is something that holds us back from the clear seeing of Lent, something beyond disbelief, even beyond despair. It is fear—fear of pain, fear of abandonment, fear, finally, of the cross itself. No human words can dispel that fear. Only the living Word of God, crucified and risen, can cast it out and lead a man or a woman through the desert into the promised land of Easter, an Easter that lies not only on the far bank of death, but in our hearts, in our cities, in those empty spaces between us.

Yet we can speak to one another the words that the living Word has spoken to us, and sometimes others will hear what we have heard, and he will set them free, too, free to feel at the mercy of pain so that they can discover that they have always been only at the mercy of God. These are words that the Lord Jesus "spoke" to me after I had spent eleven weeks one spring in the desert of a city and, even more, in the desert of my own helplessness before the immensity of its pain: "Don't be afraid. My love is greater than all the pain. I have made death itself a sacrament of life. Come. Walk into the fire." And this is what those words meant to me as I listened to them in my heart:

"Don't be afraid." It's hard not to be afraid when you think you're by yourself. It doesn't matter if you are one of a metropolitan mass of six million or alone in another sort of wilderness, if you are upheld by the warm love of a spiritual family or hidden from the eyes of the whole world. Without the knowledge of Christ's presence, not only in your room but in your heart, you will be isolated, and you will be afraid, no matter how much you may resist fear. When you are surrounded by six million people who seem isolated and afraid in just this way, the loneliness and the fear will beat at you all day long and wake you at night like the inner noise of a terrible cancer.

You will walk down street after street, and you will see faces—black, beautiful, old, ugly, sad, white, joyful—but behind all but a very few of them you will see the face of loneliness so vividly that you will want to shut your eyes or stay inside always. But even there, inside your house, inside your own head, you cannot shut out that face once you've seen it, for it is the face of Christ's image looking for the person whose heart will reveal the prototype of that image—Christ himself. That person is the one whose fear has been cast out by Christ's love.

"My love is greater than all the pain." You hear the blessed promise, and tears come to your eyes. For a moment your heart becomes as still as the heart of a child on its mother's breast. Everything in you yearns to embrace the joy of that love. But then you see the faces again, seared with pain, smeared with every substitute for hope the human brain can devise, gaunt with a hunger no food can fill. "No, Lord!" you say. "No, Lord, it's not. It can't be. Because the pain goes on and on. It has always gone on. It will always go on. You made the eye: can't you see? You made the ear: can't you hear the crying? You made the heart: don't you *know*? You must! Of course you must. You have rescued me, Jesus, and you have rescued so many others, I know. But Jesus, what about the billions of others? You are love made flesh, and if your love is greater than all the pain, where is it? Who knows you? Who knows your Mother and your saints? Your Church is a shadow. We are a few children trying to drain an ocean dry. O Lord, show us the victory of your love."

Words like that, and worse words, words that cannot even be said. And tears perhaps; tears certainly. And then silence. For a long time, only silence. Until at last a still voice speaks, speaks with such tenderness that you know it can only be his voice, and it says, "I have made death itself a sacrament of life."

The voice of Jesus stills you, finally. When you listen to it finally, it stills you. It is a voice with echoes in it, a voice whose timbre is marked forever, as his hands and his feet and his forehead and his back and his side are marked, with the sounds of his suffering in the flesh. With the loud cries and tears of Gethsemane. With the slow words to Judas, falling like rain. With the words torn from his mouth by the arrogance of priests. With the slaps on his face. With the grunts lashed from his belly and chest by the whip on his back at the pillar. With the silence chosen instead of reproach as a reed patted the crown gently, gently, and spit slid down his face. With words called forth from such clarity that they frightened the man who had never seen truth. With the dust and the growing thirst of the sorrowful way, and with the fluids and the thirst rising in the throat so that it was like drowning in sand. With lips bitten by flies and tongue swollen and clumsy against the teeth. With the echoes of the most terrible words ever said, so dark that we cannot yet tell protest from praise. With the agony of the last breaths summoned, struggling and flailing by the same energy that flung the galaxies themselves across the cosmos, summoned to say the final, gentle words that fell, at last, into stillness — where the only sound left was the unspoken question:

"O my people, what have I done to you? How have I grieved you? Answer me."

His hands glow now like jewels, and the faint white marks of healed wounds on his forehead are like a crown of diamonds. His voice, planed down to its very core by pain and made husky by death itself, is deep enough now to carry all the tenderness of the universe and infinitely more. You believe him. You believe him because you have told him what the pain does to you, and in telling you what he has done to pain, he tells you what it did to him. His knowledge surrounds yours as the sky encompasses a tiny moth.

But you believe him too because suddenly images rise in your heart, images of that kiss that turned death into life and redeemed the great angel of pain herself. You remember how one friend carried her cancer as if it were the Blessed Sacrament. You remember how another looked only faintly surprised as you prayed over her body stilled by sudden death. You remember how Fr. Eddie's face those last months glowed until it seemed that it would burst into flame. You see in faith what Mary saw in faith at the foot of the cross, and you remember the tears you have shed for others, and for yourself, and now you choose them freely.

You see them all in faith, all the millions, the billions with the single face, the seared face, the smeared and haunted face. They are walking toward him, toward the Risen One whose body is a pillar of fire and whose face is a sun, a galaxy, the face of the Father's glory. As they near him, their faces begin to lose their anguish and fear, to soften, to smile, to shine as the glory of his Father's Spirit leaps from Christ's face to their hearts to their faces—to reveal what they already truly were, to show the faces that his kiss created.

The Risen One looks at you with love and holds out his hands, and says, "Come: walk into the fire." It is all right. You know it is all right. You don't really know anything about it, but it will be all right. The anguished faces being transformed into joy disappear, fade into his radiant face—the faces of students, of professors, of mothers with their children, of workers, of those you lived with, of those you passed on the street or glimpsed on buses and in cars, the beloved faces that woke you in the night with tears, the angry faces you hid from however you could. All are changed into his face, ablaze with the fire you have wanted to see before you first opened your eyes.

You know that you will die there, in that fire, but you also know that you will finally live there. It will be all right. The Spirit has made faith bloom within you. You know that the Risen One will teach you to sing there, to sing with him the song of praise that all creation sings, to sing like the three young men in the furnace. You know that you were born to sing that song, in the heart of the fire, to become that song, that fire, wholly and yet never consuming. You see the Lovely One there with all the saints, her children, and all your brothers and sisters, and all the children of your own heart, all folded into that fire, that rose, that endless song. Above all, you see him, who is the fire, who is the song, and your fear flies away before his face, and you go to him because there is nothing in you, has never been anything else in you really, but the longing to be what he is — all fire, all praise, all love. It will be all right.

So the Spirit will lead us into the desert, into all the Lents of this life. He will open our eyes to the waste and the isolation, and he will cleanse our eyes with tears. We will grow hungry and cry out, and no doubt, the wild beasts and the demons will frighten us. It will be all right. Not only angels, but the Son of God will minister to us. The light of his face will heal our eyes, and the desert will bloom with all the children of God. We will walk together into his fire, and it will be more than all right. It will be Easter.

HOLY DARKNESS

As the western horizon tips upward, and the sun pulls its light down behind the rising edge of earth, there is a moment when blue fades from the sky and drifts instead across the ground, pooling around trees and rocks, clinging to leaves or, in winter, to every mound and flake of snow. It is the hour that, according to Tolkien, the elves call "*undomiel*," the calm pause between sunset and starshine, twilight, when our star's light is twice scattered by atmosphere and dust yet still hides the others' from our view.

Yesterday I was walking as this blue hour began. As I looked east across the fields of Carmel Hill, down to the river, and over to the hills on the other side, I had a flash of vertigo. As the bowl of the earth was turning over, it was spilling sheets of deep rose on those other hills, but even as they glowed with a last fire, the earth's own shadow raced to flood them with deep violet. How could I stand on this spinning globe? I wanted to huddle close to the ground until I could no longer see the turning, and the world had finished covering me with night.

> Our fantastic civilization has fallen out of touch with many aspects of nature, and with none more completely than with night. Primitive folk . . . do not fear night; they fear, rather, the energies and creatures to whom night gives power; we of the age of the machines, having delivered ourselves of nocturnal enemies, now have a dislike of night itself. With lights and ever more lights we drive the holiness and beauty of night back to the forests and the sea; the little villages, the crossroads even, will have none of it. Are modern folk, perhaps, afraid of night? Do they fear that vast serenity, the mystery of infinite space, the austerity of stars? . . . At home in a civilization obsessed with power, which explains its whole world in terms of energy, do they fear at night for their dull acquiesence and the pattern of their beliefs? . . . Today's civilization is full of people who have not the slightest notion of the character or the poetry of night, who have

> never even seen night. Yet to live thus, to know only artificial night, is as absurd and evil as to know only artificial day.[1]

Is it odd that I am thinking of darkness when the spring equinox is fast approaching? When the Easter dawn is only a few spins of the earth away? When I am always writing about light? But why do you think I love the sun or am searching always for the radiant face of Christ?

In the poustinia night has become my friend. Whether in midwinter, when the sun slips behind the maple bush before four, or in high summer, when it sets so far to the north that I can read without a lamp until well after nine, night falls wholly here. When it does, I can see no other lights but mine, and those in the sky, and mine are fueled with kerosene, not electricity. They burn softly and cast mild shadows on my hands, in the corners, on the large figure of Christ hanging without end on the cross on the wall. They do not compete with the night. They embrace it, and when I blow them out, night enfolds me. Enfolds, not engulfs: washed by the moon, threaded with starlight, peepers' cries, and the smell of new leaves, or even at its blackest warmed by the hidden voice of silence, night shows me its beauty nightly. Its energies, untamed, serve my solitude, nourish my stillness, promise me rest, disclose to me the other half of life. Night has become my friend here, but darkness, darkness has always been my familiar.

When I was a child, I was not afraid of the dark. How could I have been when my brother, two years younger, was afraid, and I had to be brave for him? For years we lived on a street without streetlights, with a cemetery just behind us, but night held no terrors for me despite a massive dose of "Suspense," "Molay Mystery Theatre," "The Shadow," and other radio thrillers (though "Inner Sanctum" was forbidden). Still, if the darkness outside didn't frighten me, the darkness at the bottom of the basement stairs did. My vivid imagination – or unconscious – peopled that innocent cellar with every werewolf that my daytime self denied, and if I had to go down there at night, I gritted my teeth, stiffened my spine, stayed close to the wall, and kept my eyes open very wide. I feared something, and then I was too young to know that the darkness was inside me.

I knew it was somewhere. Sometimes it showed its face in dreams, in the delirium of fevers, or even, though I didn't know it, in the despair I felt when my beloved Browns or Indians lost. As I grew, I

[1] Beston, *The Outermost House*, pp. 131-32.

began to guess that I was holding something at bay, but only when I left home and shrugged off my faith did I begin to learn that the monster crouched in the corner was metaphysical, a destiny: nothingness. I think I always suspected that the torches I thrust toward it — books, statistics, human love — were too feeble to keep it from my throat, but even without explicit faith my energies, like the fires of our ancestors during the long watches of the forest nights, seemed able to check it, to prevent it from springing. Later, after God had led me into the light, Jesus shielded me inside and out and walked with me into the lairs of nothingness. Once I ran ahead of him and lost my way, but his light in others shone in the darkness, and the darkness could not overcome him. Its energies seemed simply evil, and I blessed the Lord who gave me victory over them.

Then one night darkness sprang and caught me. Such a trivial thing unleashed it — a fear, a mood, a word, a rebuff. I felt its breath on my neck before I went to bed, and in the dead of night I awoke and knew that it had seized me, swallowed me. As I felt myself sliding down its gullet, I knew I was plunging too down through all the layers of my life, down through manhood, adolescence, childhood, down through the mind, the unconscious, the body, the spirit, down to the point of being that was the core of me. All was darkness; all was fear. I saw that I had always been afraid, and when I reached that point of darkness that was my center, where God breathed me into being, I knew that if I did not hear his voice, I would die, dissolve, vanish without a trace. I heard nothing. I was engulfed by nothingness.

But I did not die — or if I did, not as I had supposed. I got up and prayed to the Infant. I lay down again, and let the darkness have me. Eventually I fell asleep.

The next day, the next ten days really, I spent in the belly of the whale. I wasn't interested in the poetry of night or the holiness of darkness. I simply wanted to get out of this nothingness that had swallowed me. But what was it? Satan? The evil one shook my crumpled psyche in his teeth like a dog worrying a terrified fieldmouse, but once Father Callahan had prayed with me, I became certain that I was afflicted by God's silence, not by Satan's hatred. Anxiety? Of course, but when the misunderstanding that had triggered my plunge was cleared up, I remained at the bottom of the sea. An anima attack? A good name for it, perhaps, but the word seems too refined, too twentieth-century, for this primitive *thing* that had captured me like Jonah and that only God's word could get me out of. Nothingness. Darkness.

I found that day I could live with darkness; at least breathe with it. At supper someone asked me what I had been doing. "Believing," I said, and quoted John 6:29: "The work of God is this: to believe in the one he has sent." Hard work; very hard work. I was standing in the whale's belly at the sea's bottom, in my own inmost heart really, and I found myself telling God that I wasn't moving until he spoke. Maybe that was God's work? Yes: really to believe in Jesus meant to be with him completely at God's mercy, to have no other way out. So, my mind scrambled up the cliffs of fall, but still God did not speak, and I tumbled down again. I began to see that the darkness I had always feared was only another name for solitude, a companion that, like solitude, might one day become a sister and a friend.

Midnight, midpassage: the other half of life. Dante knew that the way there moved through a dark forest. Tauler speaks of a desert without landmarks, and John of the Cross writes of the night of faith. But how can this be? "God is light, and in him there is no darkness at all" (1 Jn 1:5). Christ is risen, and we are all children of the light, sons and daughters of the day (cf. 1 Thes 5:5). "I am the light of the world," Jesus says, "and whoever follows me will never walk in darkness, but will have the light of life" (Jn 8:12). Listen, though, to Psalm 139: "Even darkness is not dark to you, and the night is bright as day, for darkness is as light with you." And St. Paul understood that the only Lord, the King of Kings, dwells in unapproachable light, invisible to human eyes (1 Tim 6:16).

We are traveling into the light of God, and for us, given new eyes by the risen Lord and his all-blessing Spirit, darkness is more than an image of evil. We are not Zoroastrians. The one good God made both day and night, and his holiness is shining through his Son's cross into every space, between the galaxies or within the most tightly clenched soul, that his love has fashioned. "We live by faith, not by sight." (2 Cor 5:7). We are pilgrims into the very being of God, and our pilgrimage takes us on a journey inward toward that place where we become to our earthly eyes as invisible as he. Then, wholly transformed by the glory shining on the face of Jesus, we see our own true faces in the light of his and hear the Father speak to us his irrevocable word: "Let light shine out of darkness." (2 Cor 4:6).

Midlent: can we let the Church be a true mother to us and show us that every darkness is womb pregnant with light? And more than that; our nights are bright with God most of all because they close the poor, weak eyes of our minds, imaginations, feelings, and experiences, and open wide the single eye, the eye of eternity—faith, through which God enters and fills us with a knowledge of his love more tender and more intimate than the deepest communion of husband and wife, than ungraced angel and its creator. In this midlenten yearning for Easter can we let the Spirit show us the radiance of darkness already shining with the uncreated light?

We do not have to go out into the desert with Anthony or up the pillar with Simeon. We do not have to fast like Catherine of Siena, or go to India with Mother Teresa. Through the Church Jesus calls us instead to go, as much without fear as we can, into the depths of others' hearts, and our own, to learn that his everlasting name is "I will be there." He is going to heal every wound, turn every sorrow into joy, make every broken thing whole, mend every friendship, turn death itself into life. But we do not need to despair and flee because we see darkness now instead of light. The battlefield of my heart is littered with bodies, but as I bend over them to wipe away the blood, to keep them company until morning, or simply to weep, I sense without seeing another presence. The Living One is there. I tell the names of the earth's nations like a rosary of sorrow; which of them does not have a broken heart? Yet in their brokenness he who is the Morning Star already heralds the dawn. My own sins are trivial, unimaginative, but the tiny black hole of my egotism threatens always to suck my whole being into nothingness, and would, if the name of Jesus were not stuck in its throat, turning everything to praise.

Midlent. We are waiting for the dawn. Christ is risen, but do we have breakfast with him? The infinite Spirit fills our hearts; do we feel his fire? We are immersed in God; do we see him? In Lent, then, the Church calls us to stop fearing and fleeing our darkness, to stay with our emptiness, to let our losses take us to the nothingness of Calvary, where Love gathers all the fragments we have ever scattered, where Love's total abandonment restores all that we have loved and lost to life. It is not a matter of picking scabs, raking up the past, or stewing in the bitter juices of old pains. The Spirit leads us, rather, into the desert of our hearts to taste our creatureliness—and the good news that we need no longer fear its incompleteness. In Jesus, the Father has breathed his own fullness into every fragment of us.

As we learn to sit quietly with the Lord in the mystery of darkness, we begin to hear the fearsome names our emptiness speaks to us—hoplessness, betrayal, condemnation, abandonment, death, final nothingness, hell. We begin to sense how Christ, and often his

Mother, holds these names in his hands, gently, until their darkness is threaded with Easter, and all our poverty becomes simply a place where God himself happens to us. Rilke was right: the stories of dragons turning into princesses with the help of some brave knight were true. Everything terrible in us is simply something helpless that needs help to become right and clear at last. We are not nothing. We are only creatures, and in the night of Lent the Child of God takes hold of our creatureliness and makes it once again childhood.

"Where were you?" Abba Anthony asked Christ after the dreadful night of his greatest battle against evil spirits. "Why didn't you appear and end my suffering?" "I was here, Anthony," the Lord answered, "But I waited to see your resistance. Since you have not yielded, I will always be your helper and make you renowned everywhere." Faith: I do not know why God did not speak to me at the moment of my own deepest descent into darkness. Yet I do know that his silence has taught me how to hear my brother weeping and to embrace him, to hear my sister singing and to dance with her, to hear his own great voice in the simple beating of my heart, in the stillness of my human breathing. And when the Easter dawn rises, so will I, and then my Lord and my Father will speak to me, and I will see his light.

YES TO EASTER

Each year when March comes around I rejoice. From my childhood I remember March as the tag-end of winter. Icy winds still blew, piles of dirty snow melted too slowly on every corner, and were too often replenished by sudden blizzards. The trees remained naked, their leaves hidden in tightly clenched buds. Still, there would be days of surprising warmth, with air so clear it hurt your eyes, and as you threw baseballs back and forth, you knew that spring was coming.

But now when March comes, I think not of ragged and uncertain weather, but of the anniversary of my reception into the Church and the revelation to me of Christ's unending spring-time. I think of the Father's gift to me of faith, and each year it becomes more precious, more wonderful. I think of my coming to Madonna House for the first time, of my first Easter as a Catholic, of a joy that becomes each year vaster and more silent. I think of the words of the Letter to the Hebrews:

> And he also says, "Here I am with the children that God has given me." Since the children, as he calls them, are people of flesh and blood, Jesus himself became like them and shared their human nature. He did so that through his death he might destroy the devil, who has the power over death, and so set free those who were slaves all their lives because of their fear of death (Heb 2:13-15).

For me God's gift of freedom and life in Christ is inseparable from my life in the Church. So many these days leave the Church for what they think will be more open spaces or kinder homes, places of richer spirituality, more contemporary sorts of wisdom, or greater excitement. Many others who stay are embittered and discouraged by the events of the last 20 years. They no longer expect the Church to feed them. Most Catholics, thank God, remain loyal to the Church, and continue to rejoice in it, if more soberly and more humbly. Yet, though I rejoice with those who rejoice and mourn with those who leave or are disappointed, I do not speak for anyone else. I only know that the Church has been for me what it truly is: Christ's risen presence shining in human flesh to free me from death and the slavery of the fear of death.

It is late March, and we are moving toward Holy Week. Soon Easter will be here, but always the Church enables me to touch the risen Lord. Every day I hear his voice in the Scriptures. I was raised to respect the Scriptures, and in the seminary I was trained to search out their meaning, but the liturgy of the Church has made them the word of the living Word, as familiar and as welcome as a beloved friend's face, deeper than the universe itself. In the liturgy I learn to read and pray the Scriptures because then I hear them as the Word made flesh, actively shaping his people into his Body.

Each day the risen Christ speaks to me a word that burns away falsehood, teaches me the true names of things, and shows me my own life. In sharing with me his Name – Son, Jesus – he reveals to me my own immortal life, and in speaking his Father's love so simply to my deepest heart, he frees me from my fear that the center of me is really darkness and death. Because he speaks, I know that he lives, and because he speaks to me, I know that I live too.

Each day to the Church feeds me with the Bread of Life. In the Eucharist the Lord is as simply and as quietly in our midst as he was when he lived in Nazareth, but even more powerfully. He clothes himself in ordinariness to reveal to us our glory. "Here I am," he says, "with the children that God has given me." In every season of the year and of the heart he is present, and his life-giving Spirit touches the bread and wine and fills them with the fire of God. The first time I received the Eucharist, 29 years ago, I felt that fire and knew that by some enormous mercy I had found my way back to paradise. Now days and weeks go by so quietly that the fire usually looks like plain sunlight and the garden like my daily world. Yet always this very immersion of glory in plainness reveals to me the secret of my own flesh. My body, which will bear me down into the grave, even now, because the risen Lord shares my being, carries me beyond the visible universe into the everlasting life of God. Even now, as the sunlight becomes the image of the fire of God, my dying flesh becomes a sacrament of his life.

My death. Catherine has taught us to sing "Alleluia" when someone dies. In this as in so much else she teaches us what it is to be the Church – a family reaching beyond time as surely as it crosses cultural frontiers and national boundaries. In Christ's death the Father has claimed our life for his own and in Christ's resurrection has made our death the gateway of life. "We know that we have passed from death to life because we love the brethren," (1 Jn 3:14). The light of the risen Lord shines in my brothers and sisters, anoints my heart with his love, and makes my own humanity bright with his splendor. The very bodiliness of the Church—that earthiness that disgusts so many with the sights and smells of human weakness and sin—joins me to the Son of God, whose radiant wounds are my healing.

Through the Church Christ touches all of my senses, both inward and outward. He heals my ears, my eyes, and my flesh. He blesses my lips and loosens my tongue and fills my mouth with praise. He tells me the story of my life, and my memories become the memory of salvation. He shows me his image in the face of his Mother and of all his saints, and my own imagination is made whole. He reveals my own heart to me, and his Spirit fills my solitude with his presence until "it is no longer I who live, but Christ who lives in me" (Gal 2:20). He brings my mind there, to the place of faith, and finally, I begin to see with two eyes. March is going, and Easter is close at hand. The earth leaps into life.

This March I am haunted by the eyes of the children of Ethiopia and by the unborn eyes of millions of aborted babies. Is it possible that their suffering and death is the fruit of others' (and my own) fear of death? Is it possible that there is neither food nor room for them because the fear of death makes men and women slaves to what they own, or what they think, or what they have always done? I think that it is possible. If so, then for their sake as well as for my own, I must accept the Easter gift of freedom that the Lord Jesus holds out to me so simply. If I do not live in that freedom, in the center of me where God alone is God and Christ my Savior, then my fear will continue to bind them. My fear will bring them death, whatever else I try to give them. But if I truly "live by faith in the Son of God, who loved me and gave his life for me" (Gal 2:21), then my freedom will make a place for those children, by the power of his love.

Suddenly I see how large the life of the Church is, and how tempting it is to reject it. To receive the risen Christ, I must embrace his whole body, and if I do, my small heart and my narrow life will be broken open. What will become of me? But I know the answer to that: I will be no longer a slave, no longer even a servant, but the friend of Jesus and with him a free child of the Father.

Yes, then, to Easter, to the risen Lord, to his brothers and sisters beyond all numbering! Yes, then, to his presence in the one, holy, catholic, and apostolic Church, to the death that is also resurrection and forgiveness, to the resurrection of the body and the heart! Yes, then, to the life of the new world that is even now being born! Christ is truly risen, and the spring-time of the earth awaits only our yes.

EASTER LIGHT

Light. Light everywhere: light falling, finer than the haze of damp particles that my brother used to call "flea rain," finer than the very air we invisibly breathe, finer than a saint's heart. Light rising, more subtle and urgent than fire, denser than the night of interstellar spaces, more implacable in its kindness than that inner night we know as dread. Light: the whole universe breathes light because it is the indivisible syllable of Light that from the beginning has spoken the universe itself into life. Light: more ordinary than air, a synonym for blood, the secret face of love.

As I write, it is April, and the sun is bringing spring from the South. I tease myself with metaphors of some metaphysical south, a zone of warmth radiant enough to melt the northern darkness that seems to penetrate the world more deeply with each swing it makes around the sun. Winter has gone yet still the poor cry out with frozen voices. Still unborn babies in millions are consumed in a silent holocaust that would make an Eichmann tremble in wonder at its glacial efficiency. East and West, Right and Left shoot numbers and ideas like icy bullets at one another as labor camps and porn parlors, parliaments and universities, communes and slums and suburban homes, jail cells and revolutionary cells, hospital wards and luxury resorts are stacked with casualties like so much human cordwood. The light is shining in the darkness, but the darkness does not comprehend it.

Of course I do not comprehend it either. My mind says, "On the other hand," and my heart answers, "It's worse than that." My mind says, "Then there's no answer. It's impossible." My heart says, "It's absurd. There is no question." My mind says, "God won't let it happen." My heart says, "God let it happen to him." My mind says, "Then it's finished. Darkness." My heart says, "Light! It's Easter!" My mind says, "Absurd!" My heart says, "Now you're getting it." My mind says, "Getting what?" My heart says, "Jesus." My mind says, "Jesus?" My heart says, "Now you see!" And my mind does see, and is still. My heart says, "Won't you come home now to Easter?" And my mind does. I do.

"In him was life, and the life was the light of men. The light shines in the darkness, and the darkness has not overcome it (Jn 1:5)." So in the spring sunlight, in the world's terrible darkness, with the tears of Gethsemane on my face, perhaps forever on my face, with the hidden radiance of Gethsemane unlocked within me, let me be lighthearted, and play for you a song of Easter light.

I think at once of the first Easter I ever really knew – sunlight burning the mountains of snow away, sunlight peeling off my coats and sweaters to wash my heart and to teach it how to spell joy, daylight pouring in where just a few hours before, in the middle of the night, fire had descended to write in me the name of love. I hadn't known how hungry I was for the Bread that exploded in tongues of fire within me. I didn't know, though I thought I knew, how starved I was for the vision of the light that is the secret face of love. And not until years later did I know, though I thought I knew it then, how absolutely the fire had burned that face, the face of Jesus, into my heart that night to make my name forever a synonym for his.

But I knew his light was shining on my face. Everyone knew it. It was so clear and it so clearly revealed to me the faces of those who had already become my brothers and my sisters, that I couldn't even be shy about it. Besides, why go to so much trouble to light a lamp if you are going to hide it under a basket? I let it shine, then, as best I could when I went back to New Haven. All through that lovely spring, as my body moved through the soft May air, I knew I carried within me the Light of the world, and it felt to me that its beauty was leaving indelible traces on the streets where I walked, in the rooms and stores into which I went, and even, I hoped, on the flesh of all the people I met. But what I see now, with my memory's eye, is that the light was all around me: the fragrant mornings through which I almost danced on my way to Mass; the gray-green days of rain; the nights made harsh by fluorescents and neon; and especially the evenings when buildings and trees and sky and cars glowed with such a mellow, lucid warmth that I wondered if even Paris could shine with such intimate magnificence. God had taken my heart out of hiding and had begun to show me the glory of what his single Word had made.

I do not understand it. One moment I was in darkness, a prisoner of fear and sadness, and the next moment, thirteen months before I truly came home to the light, I was standing in what was at least the beginning of day. One moment I was busily taking notes, trying to follow the lecturer's explanation of Othello's words, "Put out the light, and then put out the light," and the next moment I was looking up at the crystalline February light streaming in the high windows of that crowded hall, and my heart was saying, "It's possible. God could exist. Faith is possible." I remember the words that were spoken then. I understand why they shattered the crust of my disbelief and revealed to me the nearness of the invisible world. I know how that dawn became sunrise very soon. But to touch that moment still living within me is to stand on the invisible line between chaos and creation and to hear with my own ears the first word ever spoken: "Let there be light!" I do not comprehend how God speaks, and I do not understand why he spoke in me, but I know that he did: "And there was light" (Gen 1:3).

Light everywhere. It has been since I've come to the poustinia, really, that I've learned about the gift of light. "In your light we see light" (Ps 36:9)—light everywhere. Sometimes, in the winter, when the moon is full and the snow is frozen to precisely the right texture, it seems as if you were walking through King Solomon's mines, with jewels sparkling in heaps, in glistening mounds, on every side. Only lovelier than that, because the air is so clear that if you listen you can hear the moon singing, and the stars, which she hides by her brilliance in the sky. Her beams scatters in the drifts at your feet, so that it seems as if you were standing in the summer sky itself, with the Milky Way breaking like surf around your feet. Or sometimes, when the moon is dark or simply the thinnest fingernail of light, you watch Orion striding through the night, Sirius at his heel, Procyon at his side, Rigel like a blue diamond in his foot, Betelguese a ruby clasp at his shoulder, Capella and Aldebaran fleeing before him, while Jupiter looks unwinkingly on and Venus slides between the branches of the trees, your eyes are so utterly full of starlight that for a moment perhaps you hear what your ancient fathers heard always: the singing of the spheres, the nightly jubilation of the stars.

In the summer the sun makes green shadows beneath all the trees and in the fields pours tons of light on every square inch of your skin. Then your heart becomes so light, so free that you learn that your skin is not a barrier as you've always thought, but a membrane letting the whole world breathe through you and carry out of you to every living thing the single word your own life endlessly speaks. In full summer nights your naked eyes can reach back two million years into the blur of the Andromeda Nebula, and you know that the gift of light is retroactive. Easter stretches back to the very beginning as well as on into eternity, and your memories become transubstantial fireflies, leading you, as once on a misty spring night the kind that fly outside your head led you, through an impenetrable curtain of darkness to the path that takes you home.

Once, riding in the observation car of a train across rainy Saskatchewan prairies, I saw the sky break open and reveal a perfect double rainbow in the East. Not an arc, but almost a full circle, it filled the whole sky we were traveling toward so that we seemed to be moving into the very essence of color. The atmosphere had become a single, enormous prism. It received a flawless, invisible whiteness and transformed it into a visible, every-colored icon of pure light that drew us into itself by its beauty, as if the train were being pulled along its track by the internal combustion of light itself.

But the splendor and the beauty of the eternal light shining through the human flesh and the human heart of Mary and then bursting forth into the crucified and risen radiance that is Jesus the Lord sheds the immortal light of the Father most of all on the human face. The sun and moon and the stars, the lights of day and night, the immaculate brilliance of winter, the glory of fall like a foresight of the whole human race at last washed clean, and transfigured in the blood of the Lamb, enrobed with the glory of God – all of these are humble lights next to the beauty of those faces over whose radiance the Father, infinite and incomprehensible light, bends with such tenderness and says, "My son. My daughter. My Beloved."

Whose faces? Our faces. Not the angels' faces, though each is a universe of incorruptible light. Our faces. My face. Your face. If you look, you will see them shining because Easter has come, and light is everywhere. It is not easy to look. Sometimes the face is so filled with pain that you know your own heart will break with sorrow if you keep on looking. It will. Sometimes the face is so twisted that you know your own body will shatter if you keep on looking. It will. Sometimes the face is so lifeless that you know you will die if you keep on looking. You will. And most of all, you know that if you try to look into your own true face, the darkness that will cover you if you keep on looking will annihilate you, funnel you into a black hole that will swallow utterly all that you seem to be. It will.

Then why look? Why shed those tears of pain? Why let yourself be broken into pieces? Why die? Why go down into the heart of darkness and disappear? One reason only, the reason your heart tells you, whispers to you in words that only you can ever really understand. Somewhere, sometime, Easter happened in you, even if it was only the moment of your conception. Somewhere, the light shone in you, and your heart knows that this light is your life. Your heart knows that if you keep on looking, you will see the face of Light, and hear his voice speak your name. Then you will live because you have heard the voice of love. Then as you name the one who is the glory of love made visible, you will see light everywhere. It will be Easter. Always.

Do you see the women weeping in the garden? Do you see the man, as ordinary as morning, question her, then speak her name? Do you see her face and feel her heart race with joy, then fall into a stillness that is perfect freedom as she fully sees his face for the first time, and for the first time truly speaks his name? Do you see Easter pass from his face to hers?

Can you see Easter happen to Peter and John, to Thomas and the others? Do you see the Easter light already shining on their faces bursting into fire on Pentecost so that they tumble out of the upper room, neither drunk nor in an ecstasy of joy, but like the every-colored rainbow, the icon of the invisible light, suddenly exploding into the sky of the Holy City? Do you see Paul's eyes, once blind, now alight with the glory of the Risen One? And do you see what he sees?

Light everywhere. "I will be with you all days, even until the end of the world" (Matt 28:20). I think of how quietly the Easter light came on last year—first beginning to gray the air of the candle-lit chapel, then awakening the birds, then showing to our inner eyes our own bodies saturated with light, then warming the air with blue, then coloring the reflections in the river, then bursting with the sun through the trees in a sudden golden "Alleluia." Light everywhere. Light: Jesus the Christ risen from the dead.

THE BREAD OF EASTER

Christ is risen! The holy night, the night of joy, the night of glory has come, and the whole creation proclaims: Jesus Christ, the Son of God, our Lord and Savior, has been raised from the dead, and we have been raised to life with him.

In the resurrection of Jesus God has poured the fire of his love into the entire universe. The one who baptizes with fire has risen from the dead, and he pours the fire of his own being upon the earth. He fills every created thing with his light so that the least grain of interstellar dust, the most momentary subatomic particle, shines with the glory of Jesus Christ to the praise of God the Father.

This is the night when those who have the gift of faith, who have received the Holy Spirit through the risen flesh of Jesus, can see the radiance of God shining on the earth, gleaming in every human face, burning in every human heart. God has baptized us with fire. We are a new creation. The old things have passed away. Death has died. For a moment the sinless one "became" sin so that forever we might become the goodness of God (2 Cor 5:21). We were lost, and now we have been found. We were dead, and now we live.

We look at a world that is still filled with pain and sorrow and death, loneliness and loss, sickness, insanity, hunger, war, and torment, but we say, "Christ is truly risen!" In Jesus God has embraced the world. In Jesus God has plunged himself into the exact center of the world's darkness. In the silence of the night God exploded into the world forever through the flesh of Jesus as he lay in the tomb. No matter what our eyes tell us remains unfinished, then, our hearts proclaim with every created thing, "Christ is truly risen!"

Above all the fire of God is alive in us. Already we have eternal life. This mortality has already put on immortality. This corruption has already put on incorruption. This humanity has put on God. If we who have been baptized with fire allow that fire to consume us, if we simply allow God in us to be God in us, then everything we touch and every person we gather into our arms and hearts will feel the risen flesh of Jesus.

As Jesus washed his disciples' feet on the night before he died, he said, "You do not understand what I am doing for you, but later you will understand" (Jn 13:7). As I watch the risen Lord bending over the world, over my own dirty feet, I do understand. Jesus embodies that line of our Madonna House "mandate," the word he himself spoke to Catherine: "Love, love, love, never counting the cost." Jesus never counted the cost. The rest of us are always counting, and our counting fills us with shame, but the extravagance of Jesus washes the shame of our miserliness away.

At the Last Supper Jesus—facing betrayal by Judas, denial by Peter, abandonment by the others, humiliation, an abyss of loneliness, dreadful physical pain and agonizing death—had no reproach in him. He told his friends what they would do to him, but without harshness, and then opened his heart to them. He loved them to the limit of his limitless heart. He did not count the cost.

What can we compare the tenderness and wholeness of this love to? Who has ever loved us that wholeheartedly? Whom have we ever loved so purely? But that we might come to believe in such a love, the Son of God does another extravagant thing before he dies so extravagantly. "Later you will understand what I am doing": we will come to know that this washing of feet reveals the meaning of Jesus's death, the secret of the Eucharist.

Years ago, before I was even a Catholic, Father Callahan washed my feet at the Holy Thursday liturgy. The next day, Good Friday, after it had been arranged that I would be received into the Church, Catherine grabbed me by the hand and led me to the sacristy, where the Blessed Sacrament was being kept until Easter. "Thank him," she said, and left. There, in that small, dark place, Jesus revealed to me his presence—and the immensity of my hunger. None of us knows how hungry we are until Jesus shows us the truth of the living Bread of Easter.

Catherine has always said, "I can endure anything between two Masses." Jesus never asks us to endure anything without his Body and Blood. Yet most of the human race seems to live without eating that Body or drinking that Blood. I lived for 20 years without that food and drink, and I wonder why I did not die of hunger and thirst. Even after I began to eat and drink, many times I did so without knowing what I did, and because of that ignorance there were many things I could not endure.

But Jesus does not stop trying to feed us. I remember an old Irish lady I visited a few times in Baltimore when I was in the seminary. She used to tell me how impossible life would be without priests. She embarrassed me, but now I know she was right. Christ is risen, but if he had not shared with us his priesthood, he could not feed us so intimately with his own life. He did not count the cost of loving his friends right to the end, and so we eat and drink his fire.

At times when you think about Jesus washing your feet and hear him tell you to do what he has done, you say, "I can never do it. No, I cannot. I can wash this one's feet, but not that one's. I can do it today, but not tomorrow. I can do it for another six months, but not for another forty years." Then you hear him say, "Just between two Masses." You begin to understand what it means to proclaim that he is risen.

Between two Masses: because Jesus did not count the cost, he baptized time itself with the fire of God's love. The time between one Eucharist and the next becomes the time of the towel and the water, the time of washing my brothers' and sisters' feet. At first we do not understand, but as we wash – grudgingly, counting each minute – we begin to discover that through this washing, in the very act of loving so humbly, Jesus is feeding us with his risen Body. As he makes the commonplace bright with his glory, our minds fall silent, and only our hearts can grasp what he shows us: that in loving as he loves us we are offered with him to the Father and are received with him as Easter bread by all those we serve.

After the Supper with his friends, Jesus went to the garden, where he said, "My heart is breaking with sorrow" (Mk 14:34). He is risen, but to live the joy of his resurrection is to experience the heartbreak of Christ. We say, "That's it. I'm finished. I follow the Lord and look what he has done to me." We are not finished, however; we are just beginning, as Jesus was. As that tiny little cramp that you thought was yourself breaks open, you discover that within there is the radiant stillness of everlasting life – Jesus himself, the Lord, with his Father and the Holy Spirit.

You discover that stillness by washing the feet of others every day. You may well only see the naked, dirty feet until, by the great tenderness of the Father, the Easter bread begins to purify your heart, and the Easter light begins to cleanse your eyes. Then you begin to see whose feet you are washing, and who is washing your feet as you wash others'. Then the time between two Masses becomes what the Mass itself is: loving sacrifice transformed by the Father's love into perfect joy. Then the Lord's word – "that my joy may be in you, and that your joy may be complete" (Jn 15:11) – is fulfilled in you because, as you let him feed you with his love and let him make you too the bread of love, your heart becomes what his heart is: an icon of that love that makes the sun rise on the good and the evil alike, that lets the rain fall on both just and unjust.

Christ is risen. He is in our midst and in our hearts, and he will be there always. His fire is burning in us, baking us. The bread is rising. Perhaps we can never stop counting the cost. But if we want – *if we want* – we can let Jesus love us the way he wants to and feed us as he longs to. We can let him wash our feet, and when we try to wash the feet of others, and fail, then we can let him feed us again, and again, and again, until his risen love puts to death in us all death, and only love remains. Then we will be the good Easter bread of God, food for all his hungry children, and we and they will sit down to feast with Jesus, our King and our Lord, for all ages of the universe and for the endlessness of eternity.

THE RISEN LIFE

"If you have been raised with Christ, seek the things that are above, where Christ is seated at the right hand of God. Set your minds on things that are above, not on things that are on earth. For you have died, and your life is hidden with Christ in God. When Christ who is our life appears, then you also will appear with him in glory" (Col 3:1-4).

"Above" is not a place. It is a life, God's life. "Our homeland is in heaven," St. Paul says in Philippians (3:20). Our homeland is God, and we have come home when at last we have no life but God's life. We live "above" when the Spirit given us by the risen Christ brings us home to the Father's ceaseless joy.

No adverb, then, can do justice to this "above" that St. Paul uses to describe the life we now share with Jesus. "Above" is not "up." The sky is up, and the sun, and the stars, and God is certainly higher, more exalted, than all these; but God's highness is not spatial. Thus God is not really up or out or beyond because he is not more present in one place than in another—except, in a mysterious way, within the human heart. Because he made us in his image and remade that image in his Son's embrace and offering of our humanity, God lives and reigns, not just past the limits of the stars, but at the center of each human being. If we accept what God has done for us in Jesus, we discover that "above" has made its home within us. We are a new creation. The Kingdom lives within.

But how are we to realize this, to lay hold of it not only with our minds, but with our lives? St. Paul, echoing the Lord himself, tells us that we will become fully what the risen Lord has made us if we practice compassion, kindness, patience, meekness, lowliness, forgiveness, and, above all, love. Yet it seems to me that the first step is faith, the acceptance of the asceticism of joy.

When the Lord greeted his disciples and friend after his resurrection, he said, "Shalom," or, in English, "Peace." He simply used the Jewish greeting, which meant "Good morning," or "Good day," or "Good evening." But what did this greeting mean on the lips of the risen Jesus? It was the proclamation of the world's healing. It meant that the whole plan of the Father had been fulfilled, that the mystery of the Kingdom lived now in the universe, that the glory of God was being poured into every atom of creation through the transformed mind, body, heart, and soul of Jesus the Messiah, the risen Son of God.

It meant that all the broken relationships in the universe had been healed at their root: that our separation from God was no more, that our alienation from one another, our enmities and misunderstandings and all our estrangements were over, that our individual fragmentation had been healed, that our separation from the animals and from all of material creation had ended in reconciliation. Jesus's greeting meant that the harmony of God's perfect order, the fullness of his life, was filling all things as it was meant to at the beginning. Easter is light, radiance, and splendor, clarity, luminosity, and brightness because it is the dawn of the new creation. It is a new day, the eternal day, and Jesus says, "Good morning."

Why do we find it so hard to say "Good morning" back to him? The answer is obvious: because we don't see this new day, we don't believe in it very deeply. We accept it intellectually, but like the rabbi who was asked why he did not accept Jesus as the Messiah, we say, "Well, when I look out the window, I don't see the blind seeing and the deaf hearing." Jesus scandalizes us, too. Even if we don't look out the window, we have only to look at ourselves to see anger and sadness, loneliness and fear, darkness and stupidity and the inability to love. Is it any wonder that we rejoice for a few hours on Easter night, but can hardly sustain it through the next day, let alone a week or seven weeks?

We lack the asceticism of joy. We laugh sometimes at our ancestors who danced for three days at a wedding and celebrated Easter for forty days. We marvel at the saints, who even in great pain were radiant with joy. But what we attribute to culture or charism is in truth due to the power of the Holy Spirit working in a heart that has truly accepted baptism. Joy is not a question of good feelings or positive thinking or even the healthy optimism of a sane self-image. It is, rather, a matter of faith, of allowing our death and resurrection in Christ and his presence within us to govern our lives—even when our actions, thoughts, and feelings stubbornly hug the earth instead of sailing gloriously "above."

If I look at the face of a man or a woman who takes the Gospel seriously, what do I see? I see someone who experiences keenly his or her own weaknesses, who carries more than an average share of the world's pain, who hears clearly the cries of anguish rising on all sides. But I also see someone radically committed to the asceticism of joy, to letting go, in faith, of his or her own darkness so that the risen Christ can shed the light of his new creation into and through the heart that God has made his home. This decision is the great vehicle of love, which is the work and the play of the new creation, because it hands over to the Lord of glory all that is still inglorious that he may make it as radiant as he is.

Some days we may be doing well if at the very end of the day we can say to Jesus, "Good morning." Sometimes we may go for weeks or months before we can truthfully say "Good day" to him. What matters is not our success so much as our striving to live in the light and our conviction that the new light is shining not because we are good, but because God has exalted his Son. The *fact* is that Christ is risen, that the world is redeemed, that the Easter sun is shining, that the morning of the new creation has dawned. If we allow our lives to be shaped by that fact, then we are leading the risen life, and the glory of Christ's joy within us is making the world what it already truly is.

Sin is everywhere, but its root is cut. Death is inevitable, but it no longer has dominion. All the evil that we experience has been lifted by the Lord's cross into the glory of God, and all of it is already radiant in his love. And in all those broken people who see only the ugliness of their pain the risen face of Jesus is clearly shining. It is for them, finally, that we are called to live in the joy of glory—that we may see their beauty and show it to them by our love. Our joy in the risen Lord, who has raised us up with him, will bring hope and healing even when we have not a single word to say to them. Reality is no longer finally harsh, and after Easter we can never go back to the normality of death. The new creation is normal now because the deepest truth is that Christ is truly risen and we have been raised up with him.

Psalm 34 says, "Look to him that you may be radiant." That is our risen life: to look to our glorious Lord, to see his death for us, united with ours for him, to receive the joy pouring forth from his throne within us, to let it flow outward in compassion and love. Christ is truly risen, and if we keep looking to him, no matter how dark the night of faith, his light will wash over us, kinder than the spring sunshine, and even our bodies will learn how to rejoice. In that joy we lose our fear of the world's pain and brokenness, and as we embrace it, it too will be lifted "above," into the glory of God. Our heart's eyes already see his light, shining on the face of Jesus, and if we live in the joy of that light, we will hasten the day when it sets blazing with praise every created thing and draws from each the single cry of victory: "Jesus Christ is risen!"

BEYOND THE BEYOND

Well, he said he was going away, and he did. He said he was coming back, and he did that too. He said that it was for our good, all of it, the going as well as the coming back. For some time now I have been wondering if I believe that.

I was always quite sure that I did. Even now, so many years later, the beauty of my first Ascension Thursday remains with me. May, of course: who could possibly have thought of May but God? It strikes me today that May was one of his more recent inventions, only possible after the earth had cooled down enough for winter to come and go, only imaginable after all those ages of swamps and ferns had given way to leaf-bearing trees and dogwood and redbud and forsythia and azaleas. But even more recent than that, really, because how could May be May if there were no mammals to feel it in their blood? In fact, could May have been before the youngest mammal of all was around to feel the breeze blowing her hair across her mouth, and laughing to smell the grass, before he was there to watch her and to catch her fragrance in his heart?

Yes, it was May and even more wonderful, Maytime in the city. An even more amazing grace there to feel the irresistible power of the earth's delicacy; to smell a green sweetness gently push aside the fumes of technological life; to see the ragged grass pressing up between the cracks of sidewalks; to taste that marvelous light on the way to Mass in the morning, or in the evening when it bathes the buildings with such mild radiance that you can almost believe that God made them too.

It was May, the time for love, and by some miracle I had fallen in love with God. Then it was Ascension Thursday, and with the whole Church I was rejoicing because Jesus was going home – and taking us with him. When, after the Gospel, the server took the paschal candle out of the sanctuary, I saw him go. I knew he was going to plunge our whole being into God—our flesh, our blood, our minds, our feelings, our memories, our hearts. Jesus was going home, and I went with him. He had taken my "captivity captive" (Eph 4:8) and filled the whole universe with his presence. How could I be sad or stand around gawking in bewilderment? God was harvesting in springtime, and my mouth was filled with laughter, and on my lips there were songs.

How could I be sad? Jesus had taken me home to God. He had gone away to give me back myself, and he had come back to give himself to me each morning in communion. That Maytime we were feasting together every day, and I no longer needed to ask him anything. I had forgotten my anguish because I was a new son whom the church had brought into the world. Oh, of course, there were bad moments and hours, papers needing to be written, people wanting explanations, a whole world demanding to know when its grief would end. But I had only to step out into ordinary sunlight to know that I was leaving streaks of light behind me as I walked through the streets tasting the world that Jesus had taken home to God and brought back to life with me. On my lips there were songs.

Whose Maytime lasts? Mine certainly didn't. The laughter ebbed; the songs faded; winter came back, many times. I forgot that I used to trail glory behind me—but not altogether. When Ascension Thursday came round each year, I always knew that Christ's going away was for my joy and that his coming back had already happened.

In fact, as my springtime fled with my childhood into the past, if anything I knew it better. "Who shall ascend the mountain of the Lord or stand in his holy place? He whose hands are sinless and whose heart is clean, who desires not worthless things," (Ps 24:3-4). As I began to understand how steep was the path to the mountaintop, how much uncleanness was in my heart and worthlessness in my desires, Ascension Thursday became for me more deeply radiant still. It became radiant with hope, a beacon on God's mountain proclaiming to me as I struggled upward that the home I hoped for was already mine, the heart I looked for I already had. What I would be somehow I already was because in his ascension Jesus had plunged me into God.

Then too, with each year that passed Pentecost was becoming more alive for me. As I descended into that strange light that seems like darkness, all those thousands of communions and all those thousands of times I touched the Body of Christ in others began to have their effect on me; and my confirmation and ordination as well, and all the tens of thousands of prayers said for me, and whatever tears and blood I may have shed. That is another story, but the Spirit of God began to show the reflection of his own hidden face to me – in the healing of my own heart, in the loveliness of the world about me, and, most especially, in the clear May eyes of Mary. And once, for just a moment on an evening when everything in me was quiet and a bright wind blew over me as I walked toward the poustinia where I live, the Hidden One breathed on my heart, lifted it above the sky, and gave it the barest hint of his own joy.

With each Ascension Thursday that comes, then, I know more deeply, if more obscurely, why Jesus went away and how he is always coming back. The home he has gone to prepare for us in God is given us by the Spirit. Here on earth, as St. Seraphim of Serov said, the Holy Spirit is the Kingdom of heaven. As that Kingdom within becomes clearer, it becomes easier to see that Jesus has not gone away at all. If he has ascended, he has ascended not so much to the Father, who is neither up nor down, in nor out, but to our own true hearts. There he lives with us rejoicing – when we receive the Eucharist, yes; when we love one another, of course; when we praise the Father, absolutely; but even when we refuse to climb further or lose our way or fall, as we think, into the pit of nothingness. "I am with you" in his *name* (Ezek 48:35), and he has engraved it on our soul's very summit.

Even more: one day you know that you are glad that Jesus has gone away because in his going the Spirit has shown you, in mystery, his face. Once I figured out how long each of us would have to wait to spend one second with Jesus if he were still with us as he was before the Father wholly transformed his humanity in his death, resurrection, ascension, and enthronement: 130 years. 130 years for a single second's meeting and a meeting is which the true face of Jesus would still be veiled! Knowing that, or sensing it if numbers don't fascinate you as they do me, you begin to rejoice to see Jesus go. You rejoice as Maytime fades away, and the old images crumble, and what seems like night descends. You rejoice with a kind of passion you could scarcely dream of at 20, even if it seems to you at times as if life's failures have taken away your Lord and you don't know where to find him. The Ascension now has become all hope, promising that Jesus is coming back, bearing with him a joy that no one will take from you, ever.

One second of his face is not enough. A billion years of his face would not be enough. Only forever, beyond all time, is enough, and so your heart rests peacefully in the darkness that is more like seeing than any seeing can now be as the calm swell of his love lifts you beyond, where he is. It is all right for now to see him no more. It is good. If he had not gone, he could not come back, and even now the not-seeing is becoming sight.

And yet. Yes, now I find those two words in my heart when I look toward Ascension Thursday. And yet for now I cannot see the face of my Lord and my God. I could not see him and live, but how can I not see him and live? It was all right for the Buddha to see only stillness – the infinity of the God he could not even name; all right for Moses to see him only in the Tent of Meeting. But God has taken a human face, the face of Jesus, and when shall I see him face to face? You, Jesus: my soul is yearning for you, my God. "My soul is thirsting for God, the God of my life; when can I enter and see the face of God" (Ps 42:2)?

My heart has said of him, this Jesus, "Seek his face. It is your face, O Lord, I seek" (Ps 27:8-9). I know I see his face, darkly, within me. I know that I see his face when I look with love at the faces of all those I meet, at the faces of those especially who are hungry and thirsty and sick and homeless. I know that, and that knowledge gives me joy. And yet. And yet all that I have learned since that long-ago May, in fact since my being was formed in my mother's womb, has taught me just one thing: that to see the unique, solitary face of Jesus, the Son of God, is the whole of my life and my joy, the whole of heaven itself. For in his face the indescribable, incomprehensible Trinity will lie open to my gaze, and when Christ's human eyes look upon me, I will see, at last, the love I was created to know.

* * *

I thought I knew how I was going to end this meditation. I was going to say that even though this knowledge of the vision I will one day have hauls me like a great rope of longing up the mountain of the Lord, my "and yet" remains in my heart. But I was also going to say that this "and yet" – this empty space, this not-seeing at the center of me – does not leave me disconsolate, but hoping in a new way that the breath of the Consoler will raise me, even now, beyond the beyond, to the place where Jesus has gone. I was going to try to say how I sensed that this new "beyond" would simply be the old ordinariness, but an ordinariness as green now and as fragrant as a new May – a Nazareth already beginning to shine with the light of the eternal city.

But a funny thing happened to me between last evening and this morning: for the first time in my life I dreamed that I saw Jesus. I had been invited to a splendid banquet, a magnificent feast where warm light shone on fine linen and rich crystal and old silver. I made my way through many empty rooms to my place. A few of us were standing by our chairs, waiting for Jesus to come. Suddenly he was there, beardless, quiet, dressed as we were. We sat and began to eat. He spoke to some of the others, and then he came to me. I looked up at him. He looked at me and spoke my name: "Bob." I think that he said a few other words to me, reassuring words, but my name was enough. He moved away, then vanished, but the blessing of his presence stayed with me. I knew that it would be enough.

It was only a dream; but somehow Jesus anointed with his own unique compassion that "and yet" in my heart. My longing drew him, and he searched me out and told me that he knew my name. He took my longing in his hands, blessed and broke it, and it became for me the bread of life.

So, once again, I can tell him that I believe that his going away is good. I can thank him for the gift of longing, which, when I eat it, lifts me beyond the beyond—to the here and now, to the reborn world, to a meeting with all the children of God, to my own resurrected heart. And if the new May is still far enough away that my mouth is not yet filled with laughter, once again as I look toward Ascension Thursday on my lips there are songs. I have nothing more to ask him—not even when.

IN THE HEART OF THE FIRE

"On earth he let you see his great fire, and from the heart of the fire you heard his word" (Deut 4:24). "There the angel of the Lord appeared to him in the shape of a flame of fire, coming from the middle of a bush" (Ex 3:2). "The mountain of Sinai was entirely wrapped in smoke, because the Lord had descended on it in the form of fire (Ex 19:18). "'Now I stand up,' says the Lord; 'now I rise to my full height.'... Which of us can live with this devouring fire, or exist in everlasting flames?" (Is 33:10, 14).

"I baptize you with water, but someone who is more powerful than I is coming,... and he will baptize you with the Holy Spirit and fire" (Lk 3:16). "I have come to cast fire on the earth, and how I wish it were blazing already" (Lk 12:49). "When Pentecost day came round, they had all met in one room, when suddenly they heard what sounded like a powerful wind from heaven, the noise of which filled the entire house in which they were sitting; and something appeared to them that seemed like tongues of fire; these separated and came to rest on the head of each of them. They were all filled with the Holy Spirit" (Acts 2:1-4).

Spring has come, and as I sit looking west across the hills where grass is leaping from the ground and leaves exploding from trees, the fire of life comes pouring down in waves of green. It blazes in every bush and cedar, in every birch and maple. It burns too in everything that flies and creeps and walks, in the little birds that wake you in the morning with their love-songs just as much as in the geese that fly north so close to the earth that you can hear the beating of their great wings as they pass. The everlasting flames, banked under the snow for so many months, have burst forth once again.

The wind from heaven sweeps through our flesh too. We burn with spring fever. We want to bathe in the sun and splash in the moonlight. Inside, we want to go out. Here, we want to be there. In the springs of Chaucer's day, folks longed to go on pilgrimage, but in our own, restlessness in May is far more likely to stimulate romance or just plain sex. In fact, we are so sure that the burning we feel each year when the green winds begin to blow is "only" human desire that we find Chaucer's pilgrims absurd, even silly. Glibly we use words like "sublimation" and "repression," and grimly or gladly prepare to treat the fever without ever questioning our culture's diagnosis. What, after all, could such tangible fire—sweeping through the belly and the heart, searing the skin—have to do with God, the absolutely intangible One?

Yes, yes, a little theological sophistication, not even very much, can make hash out of this stupidity. We are, as we say, believers in the Word made flesh, and we know that in Jesus his Son, God claimed our bodily life for his own and lifted it to his right hand. We insist, surely, that God continues to give us the Christ-life in water, bread, oil, wine, marriage and that in the end he will raise up our bodies. So we say, but have we been baptized with fire? And if we say that we have, have we seen its flames like Moses, heard its roaring like the Israelites at Sinai and the Apostles in Jerusalem, felt our skin sear with its heat? Have we groaned from bearing it in our bodies like Jesus? Has life become for us everlasting life so that spring fever and Easter joy are now a single thing—the bursting forth of the God-life in us?

I am a temple of God—really, *the* temple since God is indivisible—but do I know that the eternal fire of the Spirit is pulsing through my arteries, filling each cell of my body with such glory that the angels shield their eyes when they look at me? I know that sex and money, power and fame are merely pale images of the One who is eternal love and unbounded energy, but do I know that I am standing, like the three young men, in the heart of the all-consuming fire? I allow myself to become inflamed by hockey or politics or spring, but do I let myself think that, since Pentecost, the fire of God never ceases to pour forth from the radiant wounds of Jesus and that, if I want, I can become a living flame in that fire?

It is too much, I say, you say. I am no Moses or John the Baptist or Paul. I cannot bear that much fire, that much life, that much reality. But look: suddenly we are on new ground. Our off-hand reason for ignoring God in favor of spring, flesh, food, earth, and sun is that they are so solid, he so insubstantial. Yet let faith begin to whisper its sweet everythings in my heart, and I take the opposite tack: God is too substantial, too hot, too bright for me. "Our God is a consuming fire" (Heb 12:29): he is so *alive* that the flame of his being destroys all death in its perfect burning. In that blaze of life, that holocaust of love, would anything remain of me?

We begin, then, to get at our real resistance to Pentecost. We are not simply stupid or lazy or faithless or rebellious. For all our groaning about death, we are afraid of a life that promises to swallow up death—because we suspect that death is so deeply embedded in us that to burn it out would leave nothing, not even ashes. It isn't, then, only the annoyance of being thought drunk at nine in the morning; the inconvenience of running around dressed in camel's hair underwear; the unpleasant prospect of shipwreck and scourging; the loneliness of the mountaintop that stops us from yielding fully to the Spirit. We fear, rather, for our very selves.

God has several ways of releasing us from that fear and drawing us into his fire. We can wait until we feel our fragile lives begin to slip from our grasp, and then, with nothing much to lose, let go and drop into life. Or we can live by the energy of our own pale fire until at last, disgusted by our lukewarmness, we seek the pure heat of God's refining flames. Or like the great saints, we can betroth ourselves to the fire and leap naked into its heart.

For most of us, however, the way will be less dramatic than this; it can be straighter than the path of the weary sinner's conversion. The Lord Jesus has already baptized us with fire. It burns within us with such steadily growing heat that, like the man whom the sun charmed out of his overcoat, we need simply allow its warmth to penetrate us and draw us peacefully into its heart.

Simply: not painlessly or easily, but simply, peacefully. Look at the green fire that moves across the spring earth. Fed by sun and rain, it nonetheless arises from within. "As many as have been baptized into Christ, have put on Christ" (Gal 3:27), but not all the baptized have allowed the Christ-life within to flow forth into every part of their being—or allowed themselves to step into the wedding-chamber of their own heart, where the great Sun of salvation shines in glory. Unlike grass, trees, birds, and animals, we must *choose* our life, and choose it day by day, moment by moment. Yet it remains simple: "Lord Jesus, you knock at the door of my being from within. Come forth into my whole life." "Lord, you have baptized me with the fire of your Spirit. Now release the warmth and the light of his burning throughout all my being."

Jesus came forth from the Father to make Pentecost happen. He promised that whoever asks for the fullness of the Spirit will receive that fullness (cf. Lk 11:13). And if I receive the Living One, I will begin to live in the heart of his fire. I will know life, life in abundance, life without end. I will stand in the heart of the fire, my fear burned away, and know that fire for what it truly is: the eternal and triune love that is God made my own everlasting life.

CUSTODY OF THE EYES

Never had it, didn't want it.
I wanted bodies shining, other eyes in mine,
trees, ribbons of dawn, skies without limit,
Every-colored weather and all the faces
Leaping into my skull;
Wanted mazes of canyons, spume of stars
Whatever spiraled, flowed, or turning,
  changed;
Clouds pouring in, not puffballs
But white fires, roaring, blazing wild
Through the holes in my face, all of them;
Wanted spring earth surging into flesh,
Bark, feathers, skin – trees crazy with cold,
Jagged still with leftover winter
Arms flailing semaphores, twig-fingers
  grasping –
Mad for meeting like us all:
like me, like anyone, like God.
I wanted a seraph's ravished heart,
Not believing I'd become all eye
Unless I let my own go their way,
Unless I gave my eyes custody of me.

So I let the sun, frozen coin, hurricane of
  light,
Beat at all my gaping eyes
Even as I learned to be a priest.
Most of my brothers walked softly
Heads bowed, trusting a gift of rest
That felt to me a stone's calculus.
Even if I thought of learning stillness –

Scrubbing plank floors white
Feeling wheat fall shining, live
Nailing the world's kaleidoscope
To Jesus's heart as you walked or worked,
Letting your clumsy jumble stop
A light on still water, clear
A circle of self's repose –
I said (if anyone asked), "Let me see!
Let it come in, let me go out."

Each evening we walked alone, together;
The beads chimed in my fingers too,
Slow in the quiet fading light –
The mysteries blooming in the autumn
  leaves,
Huddling naked through Lenten Marches
Dazzling the lobes of my May-soaked
  brain –
As my eyes stalked hawks and planets,
Snatched at the bread of miracles that
  churned
By the thousand down the slopes of blue
That rose from twilight earth to heaven.
I said them, yes, believed them
Even when my chainless eyes
Came home empty, beggared, begging,
Drooling like idiots of grief,
And asked for everything, all of me.
They promised – not even mercy.

None. They hauled me out in midsleep
To nights like eternal years
To streets where April snow hushed and
  squeezed
The city to a line of pale desert,
Demanded morning for me past the stars.
Had I let my black shoes balance them
With care along the required way
God might have sooner let me see
Darkness whole, peace in my heart's
  wreckage.

But how could I recalculate,
My mind sucked out through the windows
Flung up the funnel's violence
With scrapbooks, photos, friendly rooms
  and voices
All my resting-places strewn galaxies-wide,
My yielded will hammered fine
A wire forged to pull me in
By yanking me wholly out?

Lord, I wanted the holes in my face
Open – the only way I trusted –
To the wild furnace of the sun,
To a world eaten by its own fire,
To eyes famished for wonder like mine;
But I never guessed the charred sockets,
Ears and nose burned to the bone,
Mouth blasted, endless blackened shout,
All my blood a plasma of emptiness.
I am going up in smoke.
The insatiable fuses of my eyes
Powdering my heart faster than light
Draw me bone by sinew, cell by synapse
Into the final holocaust of silence.
Eyeless, wordless, faceless I have gone.
Jesus: I begin.

ORDINARY TIME

3 THE MASTER OF LIFE

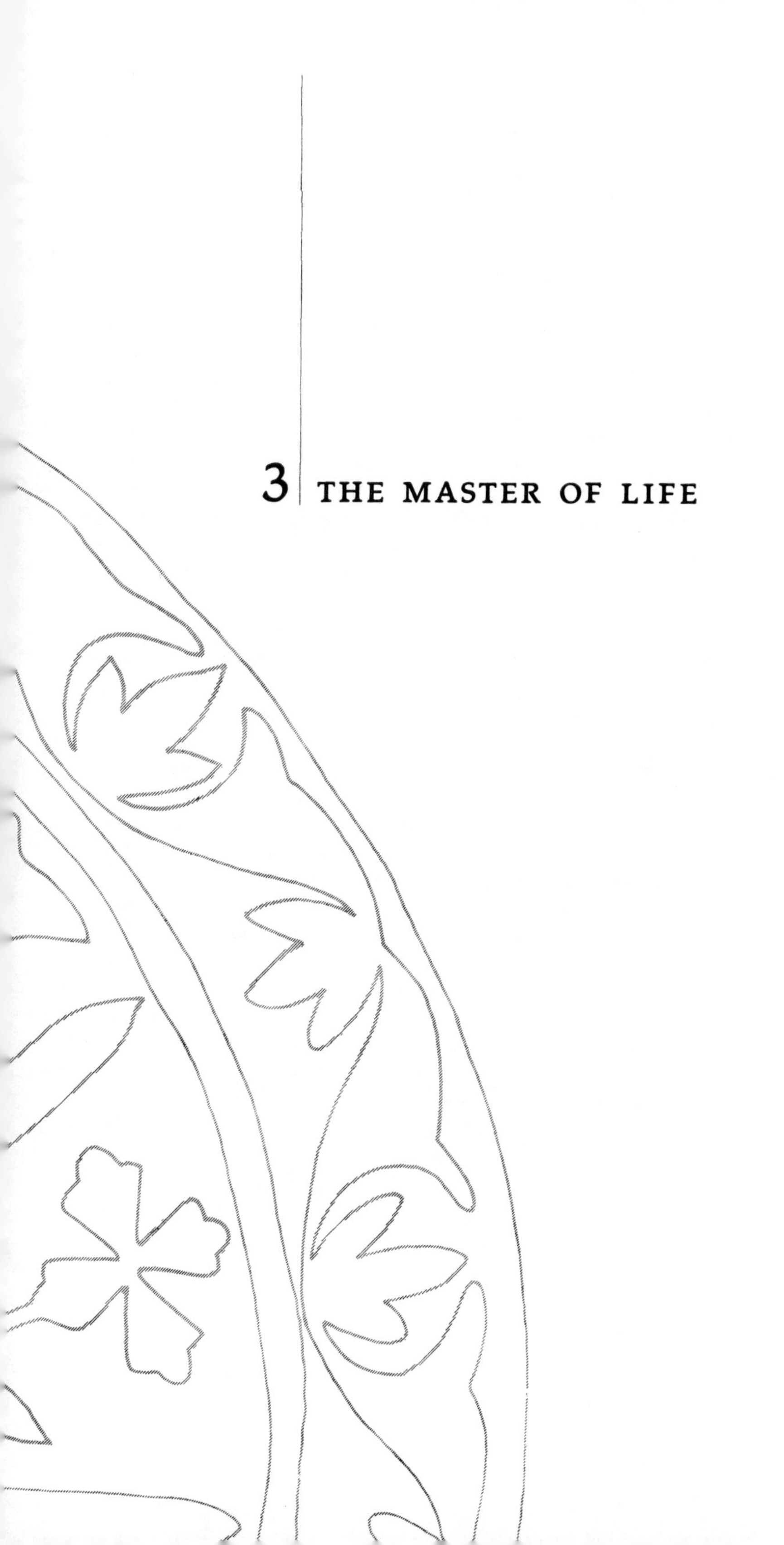

YOU CALL ME "MASTER"

On the last day of the feast, the great day, Jesus stood up and proclaimed: "If any one thirst, let him come to me and drink, whoever believes in me. As Scripture says, 'Out of his heart shall flow living water.' " Now this he said about the Spirit, which those who believed in him were to receive; for as yet the Spirit had not been given, because Jesus was not yet glorified (Jn 7:37-39).

Now Jesus has been glorified. The Father exalted him on the cross, glorified him in the resurrection, and enthroned him "at his right hand." He has given him dominion over every realm, spiritual and material, and through him he has poured out the Holy Spirit, both fire and living water, on all creation. Time itself has become time after Pentecost. Now human life is becoming communion with God in Jesus the Lord until he comes again to complete that communion and make it both visible and eternal.

The living water of the Spirit is freer than the air to flow wherever the Spirit moves, but it flows above all into and out from the hearts of the disciples of Jesus the Lord, the members of his Body, flesh of his flesh. Anyone who wants can come to him and drink, but those who have died and risen with him in baptism are called especially to see him in faith everywhere and to come to him always to drink of his life. Jesus is no longer Master only for those who might travel to see him, hear him, touch him physically. Now he is the Master who offers himself to everyone, to all who open their hearts to him and ask him to share his life with them.

But often our vision of our Master has been too small. We have thought of him, perhaps, as a teacher of doctrines or virtue, even as a minister of "graces" that help us to live what he teaches. Have we known that his words, in the Gospels, in his saints, or in his transfigured world, were giving us eternal life, the life of God himself? If not, the Master's lessons may have seemed necessary, but not the very stuff of life. Even worse, even if few besides Nietzsche and Swinburne ever dared say it, this Master of tales and intimacy, inventor of galaxies, DNA, and persons, this God who shares human blood with us, might seem to some a divinely boring preacher.

One summer day while I was in my poustinia, I leaped out of my chair and dashed outside to the corner of my garden, and stopped dead. I stood absolutely still, drinking in a scene I had seen hundreds of times before—the grass, the green slope of the hill, the leaf-bursts of the trees, the clouds, the late afternoon sun. After some minutes I asked myself what I was doing. The answer came to me simply: "I am listening to the earth." I was listening to the silence of the growing summer earth the way one listens to a master. That is the way people who saw him in the flesh or know him in the Spirit have always listened to Jesus speak, drinking him in—words, silence, presence: the Master.

Perhaps we don't know Jesus Christ as Master because we don't even know what a master is. If we knew, we might still ignore him, but at least we could not feel that his teaching is a series of abstractions or even platitudes without any real force of authority except whatever is given by blind faith, custom, or the heavy weight of "the Church's" word. We need to have our attention caught by the clear Gospel light of Jesus the Master.

Throughout the East, a master—"guru" in India, "roshi" in Japan, and so on—is a guide to life. Disciples come to him because he only teaches what he himself has experienced and because he has a personal "word" for each person who comes. The master does not teach a system. He leads disciples through various "disciplines" that bring them into the deepest truth of themselves and ultimate reality. The followers of Buddha use the tradition of spiritual mastership as a tool to guide disciples to the moment of self-extinction, where authority, self, and even spiritual experience vanish into pure silence: "If you meet the Buddha on the road, kill him." Zen masters train disciples to leap beyond linear thought and habitual perception so that they can come to "enlightenment"—a state of simple, egoless being. The true masters of the Law in Jewish life become "living Torahs." The Word of God to his people and their ceaseless exploration of it fill these rabbis with God's breath. When they speak, their followers can hear the Blessed One speaking his meticulously tender care for them.

Jesus spoke with such a voice. Those who were able to hear him, usually the sinful, the weak, the needy, or those he chose himself, heard a master with such authority that he brought health to the sick, sight to the blind, life to the dead, the good news of the Father's love to the poor, forgiveness to sinners. Yet this master was a sign of contradiction. He claimed authority over scribes, over ancient masters of the Law, over Moses himself. He claimed to be "master of the Sabbath" and "greater than the Temple." He claimed such intimacy with God that his enemies, more quickly than his disciples, saw that he thought himself "equal to God." He called all of Israel to follow him into some unimaginably new relationship to Israel's God, and to the few that did he shared the secrets of the Kingdom that his very presence was – somehow – bringing about. He refused the trappings of earthly kingship, but he died a shameful, criminal's death, a rejected King, because he knew that to "fulfill all righteousness" he had been sent into the world to master sin and death itself.

If I can say it, Jesus rose from the dead as Master of life not only because he was God, but because in his passion he had "become sin" and had been mastered by death. Jesus did not descend from heaven as the Word with all the answers. He took our flesh humbly, secretly, as he lived. But in his passing, his human flesh and human soul took God into the center of human alienation and brokenness, into the depths of human helplessness and loss. The weakness of our flesh and the rebellion of our spirit had dug a hole in God's creation – a hole in the precise middle of human life as well as at its end. Jesus filled that emptiness with his flesh and with God. Until the end of time he will teach victory over death to all who come to him, and to each who asks, he will be the Word of eternal life. In eternity we shall see him as he is – the Master who let his body be crucified, his mind, heart, and soul sacrificed, that each child of God might hear his voice, receive his Spirit, and be enlightened with unfading light.

After the resurrection and Pentecost the eyes of Jesus's disciples were opened. They knew Jesus as Christ and Lord, the Master of life. They remembered his words and deeds, and ate and drank of him at his table. They listened to his silence, and he taught them the depths of Scripture. They experienced his forgiveness, his power over all evil, his understanding of all the byways of the human heart. He taught them how to pray and to love. In the power of the Holy Spirit he even taught them how to live together in him, how to be his Church, his very Body.

The risen Master gave his Church apostles and evangelists, teachers and simple servants of the community that was the dawn of the Kingdom. Some he made healers, martyrs, and prophets, and to all he gave a growing knowledge of the sacramental life, the spring of living water that was his life in them. By the third century after his resurrection, Christ had clearly begun to shape within his Church, not only bishops and pastors, but "masters" of the Gospel life. Some of them lived in cities, but especially the great saints of the desert, mostly laypeople who had gone into solitude to serve the Master totally, allowed him to purify their minds and spirits and to draw them fully into the Kingdom that the Holy Spirit in baptism had placed in their inmost being.

These Christian masters became "mothers" and "fathers" of the Gospel life. They taught their disciples only what they themselves experienced of Christ, by the grace of the Spirit who unceasingly prayed his name within them. To those who came to them asking for a "word," they spoke a few short phrases aimed at showing the questioner the exact spot where the Master was knocking at the closed door of the seeker's inner heart. To live with one of these masters was to live in the pure light of the Gospel. This light – Christ himself – exposed sin and healed it, disclosed the paths of the inner Kingdom, and enabled disciples to return to the Master each moment of time, refined and transformed by the Spirit, that he had given them. Above all, these masters revealed in their own flesh and spirits Christ crucified and risen. They were icons of the one who is the universal Master because he is the way to the Father and because he became that way in human history by making the way of poverty, pain, rejection, powerlessness, absolute trust in God – the way of the cross – his way.

This way is foolishness to the world, but "to those who are called, ...[it is] the power of God and the wisdom of God" (1 Cor 1:24). Who is this Master that he calls all men and women to himself and lays claim over the deepest recesses of their hearts? Who is he, this Master of meekness and humility, who claims to be the good news for all of us and to each of us still speaks in the Gospel a word aimed straight at me and at you? His sayings are mysterious, elusive with depth, hard for even intimates to understand and accept. But to those who are willing to become childlike, to let themselves go and blow freely with the Spirit, his words are new life and eternal light. He teaches what he is and does what he teaches: by the wholly obedient humility of his cross, he destroys the deafness of human disobedience, and as Master of life, pours forth the living waters of the Spirit that make all men and women children of God.

It is no wonder, then, that the disciples who fully claim Jesus as Master are filled with a joy no one can take from them. As the prophets promised, they have been taught by God himself:

> But this is the covenant which I will make with the house of Israel after those days, says the Lord: I will put my law within them, and I will write it upon their hearts; and I will be their God, and they shall be my people. And no longer shall each man teach his neighbor and each his brother, saying, "Know the Lord," for they shall all know me, from the least of them to the greatest, says the Lord; for I will forgive their iniquity, and I will remember their sin no more (Jer 31:33-34).

Those who allow the Spirit-bearing word of the Master to fall into their hearts are enlightened. God has made his home with them, and their darkness has been filled and transformed by the Light. They have become the intimate friends of Jesus the Master. In the faces of all their brothers and sisters they can see his face. They are so truly one with him that his Mother has become their own, and his all-powerful Father they call, in truth and love, "Abba."

The wonder is that all of us who call ourselves disciples of the Master do not find this same joy. Yet is it a mystery? The Master speaks so clearly: "If anyone would come after me, let him deny himself and take us his cross and follow me" (Matt 16:24; Mk 8:34; Lk 9:22-27); "unless a grain of wheat fall into the ground and die. . . ." (Jn 12:24). Beyond all our struggles with faith or sin, we hesitate to become fully his disciples because we fear the cross.

If Jesus is the Master of all, then to each man and each woman who comes to him he will personally teach the secret of the cross—its joy and its victory. Yet perhaps the Master will let us hear his voice more clearly through the lives of those whom he has made masters of his way. Their lives say this:

"We came to Jesus to learn how to find God and how to show him to others. We came to him wounded or in sin, and he touched us, healed us, forgave us. He made us his disciples, and we went with him on his journeys, and he came with us on ours. He taught us what trust is and what a day is. He showed us what night is and how to pray. When we had learned all that we could learn, and were prepared as much as we could be, he began to show us the secret of his heart. He began to share with us his own compassion. He warned us at the beginning what it would mean, and perhaps we accepted his invitation to become true disciples stupidly or desperately. Where else could we go? But Jesus our Master and Lord has showed us that his compassion, the love meant to shape and fulfill every human heart, reaches its fullness only in one place, on the cross. There God cries out to God for us, and in the mystery of that naked abandonment to humble, trusting love, our own estrangement ends in peace. Where sin had made only nothingness, Jesus makes a home again for God and us to share. And he makes our own lives, with his, the bread and wine of the Father for us to share with the hungry, the sick, the hopeless – anyone at all."

The Master wants to teach us that to venture into his heart, to enter the immense passion of his love, is the new life he has to give us. Other masters give their disciples authentic spiritual gifts, but only Jesus the Master can give his disciples holiness itself – the Holy Spirit, uncreated holiness, infinite love. "The Counselor, the Holy Spirit, whom the Father will send in my name, he will teach you all things.... Peace I leave with you...." (Jn 14:25-27). This peace no one can take from us because it springs up from the heart of the one who died and lives forever – not only for us, but in us. He promises us this peace, and calls us to it, but only we can say yes. He wants us to say yes wholly.

In his resurrection Jesus mastered death and became forever the Master of life. He wants us to be where he is. With a quiet voice, deeper than all the world's noise, he calls us to master death by saying an absolute yes to the absolute fire of his Father's love. He will show us how. He will take us on the way that he is – meekness that is bold speech, humility that is freedom and love, suffering for others that is the joy of finding our own true life.

If we trust our Master's poverty, he will fill us with his Father's riches. If we accept his weakness, he will breathe in us the hidden, sovereign power of the Holy Spirit. If we embrace his lowliness, he will exalt us beyond the stars – to the place where he now stands, holding calmly in his hands the forces and energies of every possible world, visible or invisible, that as the Father's Word he made and as the Father's servant he remade.

Listen! There and here we can become listening itself – and then pure speech – as the Master speaks to us: "Come to me, and I will give you life."

BECOMING A LIVING FLAME

Most of the great parables of Jesus have slipped from our tongues and into our ears so often that they cease to bite and tease and pierce us as they are meant to do. The words of the Master, spoken to shatter our false comfort and to pull us toward the true wholeness of his Father, have instead become like coins worn smooth with age. They no longer bear the image of the one whose eyes called the rich young man to poverty and the frightened, lying Peter to repentance.

The parable of the Pharisee and the publican, for instance, Luke tells us, was spoken "to some people who prided themselves on being virtuous and despised everyone else" (Lk 18:9 ff). Yet how many of us identify with the Pharisee? Don't we see ourselves instead in the sinful, but humble tax collector, beating his breast in the back of the church? That may speak well for our honesty, but it does not necessarily mean that we have listened well to what the Master is saying to us. Is it possible, in fact, that our "honest" sensitivity to our failings might mask a different sort of pharisaic smugness? Could we possibly be praying, not with our lips, but in the depths of our hearts, "Thank you, God, that I am not like that pharisee up there, constantly parading his piety and boasting of his virtue. Thank you for the honesty and the sincerity that enable me to admit that I deserve to be standing back here, as I wait for you to give me the place you have reserved for the—well, maybe not the humble, but those who are at least *authentic.*"

It may be obvious that this sort of prayer is not what Saint Paul had in mind when he suggested that we glory in our weakness. We miss what the Lord found truly beautiful in the tax-collectors, especially since they were very likely accomplished sinners—gougers like Zaccheus, collaborators with the enemy who had conquered and exploited Israel. There is another story, however, whose strangeness may reveal the hidden meaning of the Lord's parable. It is a story taken from the sayings of the desert Fathers, those passionate lovers of Christ whose desire to live the Gospel without compromise drove them into solitude, sowed the seeds for all future monastic life, and bore fruit that still abides, even after 1,600 years, for us whose lives are so different from theirs.

> One day Father Lot went to Father Joseph and told him, "As far as I can, I keep my rule. I eat little, I pray and am silent, I work with my hands and share my bread with the poor. As best as I can, I strive to purify my heart. What else should I do?" Then Father Joseph stood up and stretched out his arms, and from his fingers shot tongues of fire. "If you want," he said, "you can become a living flame."[1]

To become a living flame: that is the Gospel proclaimed by Jesus the Master. That is what he himself is, the blazing sun who lights the whole world. That is what Saint Paul became – a libation poured out, a runner who never gave up, a weak man charged with the power of Christ, a genius whose whole mind and heart burned with the utterly foolish glory of his Lord. A living flame: what else but that is a woman like Mother Teresa of Calcutta, whose eyes are alight with the same fire whether she looks at a scrawny, abandoned baby or at the Blessed Sacrament?

There is no secret about the nature of that fire. It is simply love. Love is the fire the Son of God came to cast on the earth, and not some weak, sentimental parody of love, but the burning passion for his Father and for us that bore him to the cross and through it to his resurrection. Love is the fire the risen Lord pours into the hearts of all those who follow him, those who hear his voice today as well as his first friends.

This love is more than a human word or metaphor. It is the living Spirit of the living God, alive in us. It is the Holy Spirit who pours God's love into us and makes us living flames. If we want, then, we can become living flames of love because, as Jesus has promised, his Father does not refuse the Spirit to anyone who asks. If we ask, we shall receive, abundantly.

How simple it all is, just as Father Joseph said. Yet, like Father Lot, we are not on fire. Why not? I think that there are two reasons. The first is that we are uncertain that such extravagance is either possible or desirable. The second reason is that we are honestly not sure how to ask for the Spirit, even if we do sometimes see clearly that we can have no real joy outside the fire of his love.

---

[1]See *The Sayings of the Desert Fathers: The Alphabetical Collection*, trans. Benedicta Ward, SLG (London: A.R. Mowbray & Co., 1975), p.103.

In the story of the Pharisee and the publican, the Master is responding to this bewilderment of ours. He is telling us how to ask for the Holy Spirit. He is revealing to us the only fuel for the fire that he wants to set in our hearts. That fuel is humility. That is the clear lesson of this parable of the Pharisee and the tax-collector, but Jesus has told this story because it is much less clear how humility joins together simplicity and infinite depth. Most of our notions of humility are loaded with the baggage of self-hatred. The Master wants us to see that humility has nothing to do with self-hatred, partly because our sinfulness is so unsurprising, but above all because the Father's goodness is so endlessly, spectacularly surprising. The Lord wants to teach us how to be humble, by telling us the truth about our own wretchedness as he reveals to us the greatest truth – the truth enfolding and encompassing every other truth – that is the mercy of his Father.

The Pharisee stands before God secure in his own right-acting and right-thinking, and does not meet God at all. The tax-collector stands before God in utter poverty, with empty hands, and he meets the God whose deepest name is mercy and tenderness, who delights to call himself our Father. The Pharisee thinks that he sees God's face in the good order of his life, but he sees only his own narrow heart. The tax-collector sees only his own poverty, and in that emptiness God shows the beautiful face of his mercy. Father Lot led a life of true justice, yet he knew something was lacking. Father Joseph stretched out his arms to heaven and showed him that, beyond the careful country of Father Lot's rule, lay the bright, clear air of the Kingdom, the boundlessly open space of God's passion to clothe us with his own splendor and to fill us with joy of his own freedom.

Thus the Master is teaching us that humility carries us into the kingdom of love because humility is the living knowledge that the mercy of God is our true environment. We always want to live somewhere else – in the security of wealth or power, in the safety of our own intelligence, in the false peace of our own ego-strength, behind the walls of our good works and right opinions, in the house built by the esteem and approval of others. But Jesus is teaching us that we have no home except in the mercy of God, that outside this home we are fish flopping on dry land, birds trying to fly in water, children trying to learn the language of love without parents to teach them. Everyone who tries to build his own life will see it collapse, but whoever dives into the mercy of God will be lifted into glory.

There are good arguments against a life lived like that: it is too risky; it is too childish, not risky enough; it is too difficult to be that simple; it is too demeaning; it is all too likely to end in a false peace that ignores the injustice of the world and the pain of the poor. However, the overwhelming argument on behalf of a life lived in total dependence on the tender love of the Father is Jesus himself. In him there was no sin, yet "he became sin that we might become God's goodness" (2 Cor 5:21). He was equal to the Father, yet became poor that we might become rich, and now his poverty and his Lordship are one. He is the wholly meek one, yet who has ever been more free? He is God's own fool, yet who has ever been so wise? He is completely the Father's Son, the eternal Child, yet who has ever been more adult? He refused the chance to become an earthly king or a political revolutionary, yet he built with his own body a kingdom of justice and love for all the poor.

In the end, we must simply decide if this way of Jesus is opium or the very bread of life. This is a question addressed every bit as much to those who consider themselves conservative as it is to liberals or radicals, for it is not just some sort of political styles or social structures that the humility of the Master reveals to be inadequate, but all of them. The pattern of order as well as the wellspring of freedom, the source of human justice as well as the origin of humane social processes—all begin in the act of truth that accepts God's mercy as home and asks his Spirit to consume us as Jesus was consumed for us and is consumed by us in every Eucharist.

Our Lord and Master has made himself our food and drink as he has made himself our fire and light. If we remain inconsolable until our own prayer pierces the clouds and the Father makes us also living flames, the reason is that our burning is ultimately for others. Everywhere our sisters and brothers are dying of hunger, cold, and disbelief. If we refuse the humility of Christ and the fire of his love, who will feed them or warm them—or light their way home to the tenderness of their Father?

ABIDING IN GOD'S HEART

The first time I saw a picture of the Sacred Heart I was six or seven. It seems strange how vividly I remember it, though the only thing I remember about the people in whose house the picture hung is the pale, sweet, Irish face of the mother of the family. Strange is the word all right: there it was on the wall, a framed picture of a human heart surrounded with what seemed to be barbed wire. And right beneath it was the picture of another human heart, this one pierced by a sword. No faces, no bodies, only hearts.

Did I really ask what they meant? I think so. Curiosity overcame shyness, and someone answered my question very simply: "That is the Heart of Jesus, and that one is the Heart of Mary." Obvious? Not to me. I knew the names, but the pictures might just as well have been images of Hindu deities or Buddhist *arhats* for all the familiarity they conveyed to me. They were not grotesque or bloody; only strange, alien to my world even though my house was only two doors away and these pleasant people seemed just as much at home on our street as I was.

My grandmother used to say, "Bless your heart." I never asked what she meant. It was simply something Grandma said, like "Pshaw!" when she was vexed, or "machine" for car, or "Are you sick?" when you refused a third helping of her good food. When she blessed my heart, I knew that she wished me a kindess. I know that I grasped that much, though I had no idea really what my heart was, or why she or the kind God she believed in but didn't directly invoke would want to bless it. Well, perhaps I did understand, a little. Surely I knew that it meant she liked me, but then a lot of the things she did told me that – such as not insisting that my brother and I eat the whites of soft-boiled eggs, or being convinced that our squeaky singing voices were beautiful; or thinking that I was the smartest thing on two legs.

It feels right to say that my grandmother liked me when she blessed my heart. I assume that I heard the word "love" fairly often, but I knew very clearly what "liked" meant. It meant that you were cared for, and more than that: *enjoyed*. Even later, when childhood romances began to bloom, we always said "liked" when we wanted to explain why someone was taking such a special interest in someone else of the opposite sex. As for example, "Connie likes Eddie," or "Dale likes Maggie" (and he washed my face in snow because I liked her too). I didn't know what that sort of liking had to do with the heart either, but my old notebooks were full of wavering Valentines inscribed with various initials: B.P. and R.K., B.P. and J.L. And certainly: B.P. and S.O.!

Dreams of innocence, yes, but not free from pain. Not at all. The books I read—fairy tales, stories of pioneers—spoke often of broken hearts and of people pining way into early death. I remember musing about this secret wasting—as dreadful as cancer, as relentless as old age, as violent as war. What was it, really? Did anyone outside of books, beyond the world of the imagination, catch it or get caught by it? I wondered about such things now and then, but never linked those paper tales of inner pain with the heart that my grandmother blessed, or with those schematic images, unbloodily pierced by an arrow, which I drew to enclose and embody somehow my liking, or with the anxieties that sometimes gripped my chest or stomach. Certainly I did not link any of these archaic languages with the picture I had seen one day at six or seven. Or with Jesus at all.

Yet in that very heart whose reality was apparently only a puzzle, and a not very interesting one at that, I must have been pondering these things, pressing them this way and that for meaning, because the very night when I at long last "saw" that the Church was the Body of Christ extending into all time and space, I thought at once of the Sacred Heart. The instant I knew, and knew with a certitude that came from the very root of my spirit, that Christ was still physically present in the universe, I also knew that at the precise center of that presence was his Heart. I did not think it; if anything was ever revealed to me, that was—the body of Christ present always, fueled forever by the divine energies of his Father's inexhaustible love, eternally fashioned and re-fashioned by the Spirit out of the inmost place in the Son where God and man are joined forever.

Since then, I have spent my life exploring the limitless terrain of that mysterious place—which is really no "place" at all, but simply the center of the being of the Word made flesh, crucified, risen, and glorified. It is so vast that is usually appears commonplace. It is always unpretentious. Much of the time I haven't even known what I was doing, that I was *there*. It is easy to understand how his neighbors asked in peevish bewilderment, "Isn't this the carpenter's son?" Being there, being with Jesus, being loved by Jesus, being immersed in the Father is mostly so ordinary that you keep muttering, or complaining, "But it's just life!" Yes. You can try to understand that ordinariness if you want by analyzing the nature of the baptismal seal or by probing the meaning of the stages of prayer. Or you can let your mind burst into stillness by dropping into it the simple question posed to me one summer by a sister from Africa: "Is it possible to be half-way to God?"

Is there any other question than that? As I listen to what I ask and what others ask me, it seems that all our asking is answered by this single question. We ask: "How do I find rest?" "How do I discover my heart?" "How do I know, really know, that God loves me?" "How can I see the face of Christ?" "How can I learn to be still, simply to be?" Charismatics say, "Praise God!" Catherine says, "Fold the wings of your intellect and open the wings of your heart." St. John Climacus and the monks of the Christian East say, "Remember Jesus with every breath." Or, as the Master himself said to Pascal, and through Pascal to me on the day following the night when I first saw the meaning of his heart: "You would not be seeking me if you had not already found me." Is it possible to be half-way to God?

We are speaking here about faith, about the power the Spirit gives to the mind enabling it to assent to the truth, and more profoundly, about the *life* the Spirit pours into the heart empowering it to see the invisible, to touch the intangible, to be present to the one who is eternal presence. The Master has chosen to stay with us, to abide in us. When I consider that staying and that abiding, it always manifests itself to me as stillness. If I look into the face of an icon, or if I imagine the eyes of Jesus as he walked on a street in Capernaum or planed a piece of wood or hung on the cross, I see stillness. If I think of his love, I am touched by stillness, a deep river flowing all through me. Or if, beyond all images, I only say his name, my own heart becomes still, and I am immersed in his stillness. "In your light we see light" (Ps 36:9): in his stillness we become stillness.

What is faith, finally, but the choice of this stillness, the choice to wait? "He trusted to wait till the secret of leaves, if nothing more, came into his power. First the power to watch one green leaf in stillness; then the dark banked branches in all their intricate shifting concealment – concealed good news (that under the face of the earth lay care, a loving heart)."[1] That is how a novelist speaks of the act of the heart that chooses its own fulfillment in patience, in passion transformed into the concentrated awareness of a leaf – the growing edge of life.

Faith accepts that the promised life has already been given us. It is an act of loving trust – simpler than planting a seed in the earth, more daring than waiting for the universe to bring forth what lies at its core, even more basic than letting one's infant self be mothered – that Jesus wants to be fully Jesus for me: Master, Savior, face of the Father, breather of the Spirit, heart's true food. If I embrace the stillness of my Master, I discover that the door at which he was standing disappears, that we are already dining together in the intimacy of evening, that God has become God-with-us. Already.

"The word heart is used in Scripture," the old Cruden's Concordance says, "as the seat of life or strength; hence it means mind, soul, spirit, or one's entire emotional nature and understanding. It is also used as the center or inner part of a thing."[2] In other words, it is the heart that embodies and expresses something's or someone's true being. "At heart he is very good." "I have your joy at heart." "You are a child after my own heart." "She wants to live with all her heart." "I am speaking right from the heart." "Blessed are the pure of heart." "Mary kept all these things in her heart." "Learn from me, for I am meek and humble of heart."

"Whoever sees me sees the Father," Jesus says (Jn 14:9). "He is the image of the invisible God" (Col 1:15). "And the Word was made flesh and dwelt among us" (Jn 1:14). The eternal expression of God's inmost being has come forth into human life. God has revealed his heart, and that revelation is Jesus. Jesus does not simply have a heart, a humble heart, a Sacred Heart: he is the Sacred Heart, the Heart of God expressed forever in human flesh.

When I wait, when I become still, when I let all my questions draw together into a single question – "Is it possible to be half-way to God?" – and let that question too fall away into silence, I hear a single word: Jesus, the heart-beat of the living God, the pulse of my own true heart. Then out of this simple awareness that God has already become God-with-us, as calmly as the sun rises every morning, as amazingly as a blossom becomes an apple, as irresistibly as a

---

[1]Reynolds Price, *The Surface of the Earth.*

[2]Alexander Cruden, *Cruden's Complete Concordance,* (Philadelphia: John C. Winston Company, 1930), p. 290.

child grows, comes the knowledge that God has freely chosen to be with me. He knit me together in my mother's womb. He saw my face before I had a face. Before I was born, he pronounced my name. Long before I knew what a heart was or that I had one of my own, he blessed my heart. Before I could write, he wrote my name in his heart. When I had not even one word of praise to give him, he chose to give me the Word of his pure delight. He made me his child. He likes me.

And when my heart broke, he held the shattered pieces in his heart. When there was no resting-place for me, and I roamed the little universe I knew looking for someone to rest in, anyone but him, he still rested in me, without blame, without regret. When I said sometimes yes and sometimes no to him, he was always yes to me, even when my deafness twisted his yes to no. When I was more than half in love with death, he was altogether in love with my life so that, when at last I exhausted my store of self-contempt, his inexhaustible care for me became my heart's ease. My joylessness had turned the whole world gray for me, but his joy in me was always green until the day I became humble enough for laughter instead of tears. Since then, even when I did not know it, even when the mysterious logic of joy led me to the roots of all my tears, I have been exploring that place, which is no place at all, where God's delight becomes human life.

Once, several years ago, during a day spent in poustinia, it occurred to me that Jesus stood at the door and knocked. In a burst of childlike literal-mindedness I went to the door of the poustinia, yanked it open, and began to bow. The blast of joy that exploded through that open door knocked me to my knees. For a few moments I knelt in the center of the sun, and then all was back to normal: a dull October day, a little room, a poor man. There was no vision, no ecstasy, perhaps mostly illusion growing out of needy feelings. But that poor man learned something that day about the risen Jesus: his joy is vaster than the cosmos, stronger than death.

When I think of the summer feast of the Sacred Heart, I see always a June day nearly forty years ago when ordinariness was tuned almost to a perfect pitch. The sun on the full fresh leaves and on my shoulders as I rode through the morning delivering my papers was like a promise fulfilled so dazzlingly that the anxiety of waiting utterly vanishes. The air, the sky was as clear as Mary's heart, and the birds sang, I sang, songs better than songs of Eden never lost: songs of Eden refound. It was an apparently perfect day that, in a flash, became truly perfect. As I wheeled my bicycle up one drive, kicked down the stand, pulled out a paper, and started up the steps, a woman dressed for Saturday cleaning or gardening came through the door and took the paper from me. I don't remember who spoke first. We spoke only simple words: "What a nice day!" "Yes, it is!" Her whole being smiled with mine. After all these years, after so many other days, I remember especially how happy the day had made her too, how happy it made us both to share our delight for a few seconds, how fine it tasted, shared, like cool water, like bread and wine.

So perhaps I was wrong. Perhaps I first saw a picture of the Sacred Heart, not at six or seven, but much, much earlier, in my mother's love and in my father's. And perhaps I did know what it was, somehow; perhaps I have never known anything else. Certainly it feels that way whenever I come home to the joy of Jesus and to the mercy of God that shines there. Certainly it seems so to me as I taste the delight of God, and see it is the food I was born to eat. Certainly that is what my heart says when it is still and resting in the Master's heart: that God has only this one expression, one Word, Jesus, and that this single Word of joy is simply love. His invincible love lies waiting to burst into flame at the center of all things, already makes its home in every human heart and shines with secret Taboric splendor on every human face. "Listen – learn from me, for I am meek and humble of heart" (Mt 11:29) – and you will find that it is impossible to be half-way to God.

WHOEVER HAS EYES

Seeing is not believing, as Christ often pointed out to those who looked at him only with their physical eyes. Nor does faith come simply by letting certain bits of air shaped by throat, tongue, and teeth pass from a master's lips into the subtle workings of a disciple's ear and brain. Seeing and hearing—the new faith of real conversions—happen when someone sees a sight or hears a word that startles, awakens, enlightens. Perhaps not suddenly, but in any event *now, his* life, *her* life is something quite other than he or she has known before. Realization or true awareness is an act of one's deepest being.

It has often occurred to me that most of us for much of our lives, and some of us for all of our lives, huddle in a prison like bees in a frozen hive. We exist inertly, enclosed in dark, cold cells. We spend our days (and even our nights) groping around the walls, inventing new routines for ourselves, building little monuments of "meaning" in the corners. At times we sit, paralyzed, in a stupor of loneliness, afraid that our cell is all that exists; at other times we tap out coded messages on the walls or try to burrow through them to others or even batter the ceiling with prayers. Sometimes we rage at our separation from wholeness, or distract ourselves with food and chatter, but most often, believing in God somehow or another, we work to dismantle our cells stone by stone. All the while, the truth is that the Lord Jesus Christ has ripped the roof off our frozen hive, and the new sun is pouring in.

The voice of the Gospels is like the urgent summons of John the Baptist, a voice thrusting at our ears, plucking at our eyelids, insisting that we let in the light of the risen Lord: "Christ is risen! Look! The roof is gone! He is risen! See! The sun is shining. The walls have fallen. You can open our eyes. You can walk out of your prison. Listen! The Lord is speaking to you. You can go anywhere. You can be as free as Jesus—as free as God."

To live as Jesus Christ lives—Christ risen from the dead, Christ who sets prisoners free: what does that mean? "Go," the Lord says, "and learn the meaning of the words, 'What I desire is mercy, not sacrifice (Mt 9:13).'" Samuel told Saul that God wanted obedience, not sacrifice (see 1 Sam 15:22ff.). It was a hard saying. God had commanded Saul to destroy the Amalekites utterly, along with all their animals. It was bad enough to kill even the women and children, but why waste even the animals, especially those that could be offered to God? Saul thought he knew better than God how to be a successful king, but God did not want Saul's ideas or Saul's animals. He wanted Saul.

Saul never quite got it. David did, though, almost in spite of himself and the temptations of power. But God knew that if his people were ever to learn obedience, he would have to teach them what it meant to offer their hearts to him. God used the prophets to teach Israel and the world divine mercy and humble, human trust. He used Hosea to deepen the words of Samuel: "What I want is love"—steadfast love, mercy—"not sacrifice, knowledge of God, not burnt offerings" (Hos 6:6). I want you, God is saying, to sacrifice your heart to me, and that means more than any sacrifice of gold or silver, oxen and sheep, because if you give me your heart, I can give you mine.

We Christians often miss God's meaning because animal sacrifices seem senseless to us. Yet if we had ever seen the total reverence before the mystery of the Holy One of those we call "primitive," we might realize that in our entire lives we had never performed a single act of worship as wholehearted as the everyday sacrifices of peoples who know what awe is. In a similar way, we tend to scorn the obedience of Orthodox Jews and mock their observance of the Law as pharisaism. But we can learn from the Jews about obedience, about the passion and the joy they pour into doing what God has told them to do, no matter how small, obscure, or inconvenient.

Nevertheless, God has said, "That is not enough. Sacrifice is not enough, just as outward observance is not enough. I want you to sacrifice your heart to me always, in everything. You think that you want to do that? You think that you know what I want? That you *know* me? Then go and learn what it means to take care of the helpless—the poor, the widows, the orphans—and then you might be ready to know me."

Jesus came to reveal the full depth of God's word. Eternal Wisdom in human flesh identified himself so completely with the poor and the helpless that merciful love given to them would at the same time bless Christ himself — and make its giver one with him in his Kingdom (see Mt 25:25). Yet Wisdom is deeper still. It is one thing to give merciful love to widows, orphans, and the poor; it is something more to give it to petty gangsters and prostitutes, to pushers and porn kings, to all the smiling, cold-eyed politicians who milk the poor, to the men of power "whose eyes swell with fatness," to the truly evil who worship violence and say, "How can God know?" (Ps 73:7-11). Most of us have enough difficulty believing that God will show mercy toward the kinds of sin we wrestle with — pride, lust, enduring resentment. What do we make of the Master's mercy, not to those who deserve it, but to those who don't?

"Go and learn the meaning of the words, 'What I want is mercy, not sacrifice.'" Do we want to have a heart that is a holocaust? Do we want to be with Samuel or with Saul? Do we want to be with the prophets, who told the mighty to repent and then died for them? Do we want our hearts to bow to the dust with Wisdom in the flesh, the Master who forgave his enemies as they were killing him? Then listen to him: "Go and learn the meaning of the words, 'What I want is mercy, not sacrifice.'"

It is a hard lesson, harder than Saul's. When the Pharisees came to Jesus as he ate with tax collectors and sinners or allowed his disciples to pick grain to eat on the Sabbath, he told them that if they had understood God's words to Hosea, they would neither despise the guilty nor condemn the innocent. It is a hard lesson that Jesus teaches, a lesson that we resist as much as the Pharisees did. The Master is teaching us the sovereign freedom of God's merciful love.

God's love is not bound. There is order in God, but it is the order of Father, Son, and Spirit communing in inexhaustible love. Infinite being is infinite, boundless love. The laws of the universe come forth from that love like rays from the sun. Whether physical, moral, or spiritual, they are splendid as they hold all created things in being and ground them in the One in whom "they live and move and have their being" (Acts 17:20). Some day we shall see all the energies of creation woven into such a perfect system of intelligence and beauty that we shall burst into a song of praise with no pause or end. But God is not bound by that system. That system is not God, but only a magnificently humble image of his merciful face.

Yet what are we to make of this boundlessness of God? Does it mean cosmic anarchy for us very bounded human persons? What if the force of gravity no longer holds? What will I do if the atoms of my body split apart? What will happen if the sun does not shine, if summer never comes? What if water no longer quenches my thirst or my blood literally starts running cold? And what will happen if, in imitation of all this chaos, men and women too take the law into their own hands and begin to do just as they please? Can the result be anything but death? How can God be beyond law if his "freedom" builds anarchy into the very fabric of his creation? "Go," the Master says, "and learn the meaning of the words, 'What I want is mercy, not sacrifice.'"

It is a hard lesson indeed. Do we want a big God, a free God? Do we want the real God? Do we want him to be able to sit down with sinners and have a good time? Perhaps we do. Perhaps it may not be too difficult to begrudge God a party, and perhaps we might even let go our metaphysical as well as our moral terrors and admit that only a truly transcendent God could make a universe both as ordered and as random as ours clearly is. But what God's generosity implies for the ordering of my own here-and-now life is far more unsettling than any intellectual debate. The Master may be talking to the Pharisees, but he is looking at me, and he is demanding of me a heart as big as God's—shining on the just and the unjust, pouring compassion on those who like me and on those who mean me harm, patient with the foolish as well as the wise. He is disarming me. After so many years of learning obedience, after so much healing and hard work to discover that my life does not depend on the approval of anyone else, am I supposed to put my heart in the dust for anybody to walk on? Do I want to be that big? Can I stand to live so freely, with so much faith? If I try, I'll end up splattered on a cross like Jesus.

Jesus: Jesus the Master shows us what it means to live in mercy. He says, "Lose your life so that you can find it. Come with me and live. Work with me, walk with me, sit still with me. Be with me, and I will teach you how to live in grace. I will show you how to receive the Father's love. You will become little and poor with me, and you will be made invincible with me. You will find joy. You will live forever."

So often we answer, with great longing in our souls, "Lord, it is great—too great. I can't. I can't be that forgiving, that free, that trusting. I can't walk up the hill with Abraham. I can't endure with St. Paul. I can't let you do with me what you want as your Mother did. I'm sorry, but I can't."

Then the Lord says, "I know it. I know that you don't know me well enough yet. As you turn that corner and say goodbye to me—maybe for five minutes, maybe for five weeks, maybe for five years—you are going to think that you have gone away from me. But I want to tell you that you haven't, that I am with you. Do you know what my cross means? It means that I have gone with you into all those places where you think you are without God. I have gone with you there. I have cried out in agony with you there. I have bled with you there, and sweated with you there, and I have known your loneliness and embraced the darkness of your fear. There is no place where you can go where you are wholly outcast because I am everywhere. Sacrifice and obedience, mercy and love have all met in my heart. Where you are, I am. And I will be there always. I will never let you go. There never will be a place where you go—never, not ever—that I am not with you. That is the meaning of the words, 'What I desire is mercy, not sacrifice.'

"And even if you think that you have gone into hell because you are so far from me, I tell you, you are not far from me. I am with you because I am the Lord. I have died and have risen as I promised. The Father's mercy is greater than all things, greater than every law, than every form of death, than every created thing. The Father's mercy is without end, and I give it to you always, without measure."

This is the life the Master calls us to. In the end our hearts, our inmost souls, tell us the truth: we do want to end up like him. Perhaps we will never understand the cross. Maybe we will never like what it proclaims about pain and blood. But to whom else shall we go for life? And so we say to him, "Lord, yes, I want to be with you and become like you—risen and free, unafraid, radiant with the knowledge of mercy."

Then Jesus looks at us with love and says, "Follow me. Watch my steps. I will teach you how to dance."

As we let go, as we forget to be embarrassed or afraid, we discover that mercy is a dance, even the pain of it, because what is it, finally, but infinite love made visible? Where else could we find joy? In the middle of life here and now—whole or scattered, running to Jesus or away from him, knowing him and not knowing him—the Master teaches us the dance of true blessedness. "This is my body," he says, "and this is my blood. Taste and see that I am life—and that I have come to live in you. Taste and see who has made himself your Father."

As we do, we see too that we have leaped out of our prisons into the clear, free country of God's unbounded mercy. It is morning, and the sun is huge on the horizon. Wildflowers are everywhere in the green summer grass. There will be time for everyone and everything. We are going home.

THE TRUE FLESH

"I am the living bread that came down from heaven.... This bread is my flesh, which I will give for the life of the world.... Unless you eat the flesh of the Son of Man and drink his blood, you have no life in you. Whoever eats my flesh and drinks my blood has eternal life, and I will raise him up at the last day. For my flesh is real food and my blood is real drink. Whoever eats my flesh and drinks my blood remains in me, and I in him" (John 6:51-57).

Is it any wonder they grumbled? Is it surprising that they found his language intolerable? Who can bear it, even today? Isn't that the question that bites at our hearts just as sharply on sweet afternoons in the sun as in the grief of sleepness nights? The question, that is, whether the Master really knows what he is talking about. Does he know his own business? Does God—never mind in theory, but in practice—know how to be God?

We look around and see Ethiopians starving (a few years ago it was Bengalis and Cambodians; next year it will be someone else), the Middle East a cauldron, Afghanistan a crucifixion, children by the million weeping everywhere, beaten, abandoned, lost forever to happiness on this earth, men and women in bondages desperate and sad beyond any possibility of tears, the Body of Christ, the Church, bleeding from how many thousands of wounds. We look within, and even if—especially if—we know that the risen Christ shines in us, we see, beyond sorrow or joy or fear, beyond even sin and egotism, an abyss of loneliness plunging into the bowels of being itself, a hole so big that all the matter in the universe could not fill it up. Does God know how to be God?

The heavens burst open quietly. The Son of God comes to us, eternity strolling in time, everlasting light with a human spirit, human innards, human bones, human face and human skin getting burned by the earth's sun on the dusty little roads of Palestine. God is made human flesh, and with a wholly human voice the single Word spoken by God cries out, "My flesh is real food, and my blood is real drink."

How can we help but say, "What is he talking about? How can he give us his flesh to eat? What is this? Are we cannibals? His flesh? The Romans – or the rich or the Russians or the proud – are standing on our necks. Will his flesh get them off? My little boy has cancer, my wife is having an affair, I am old and tired, my heart is broken: What is this about blood? I am going to die, am dying now, my own flesh falling into dust, already crumbling into darkness. How can this food – too gross to eat, too subtle to understand – save me?"

God seems either too far or too near. He lives above the galaxies, beneath all we might hope to touch with our minds. Then he comes to a green hillside in spring and speaks these baffling words that rouse our half-buried longing to see, somehow, ourselves – someday all of us our whole selves – absolutely alive. Job sat in the dung and insisted that his own wept-out eyes would one day see the living God and be satisfied. And so God comes, and he says to us, "My flesh really is food. My blood really is drink."

His words break our hearts with longing. Can any of us believe anything finally that is not in the flesh? Buddhists and other Orientals and our own great saints may pass beyond desire and passion, but do they leave their bodies behind? As for the rest of us, we simply know that our flesh is inescapable. It is as unalterably *here* as the earth, and it is never right – too much or too little, too insensitive or too painful, not beautiful enough for anyone to cherish or maybe even so lovely that others devour us. It is here. Our flesh is us. Could we ever possibly have a God who would not touch us in our flesh?

Jesus multiplies the loaves and fishes, heals the wreckage of our dying bodies, and then he looks us right in the face, and his voice pierces to the center of our hearts' flesh as he says, "My flesh is the true food, and my blood is the true drink." He is asking us to open our flesh and our spirit to the food that will truly fill us.

Could we ever believe in a love that would not embrace our flesh? Those who follow Christ strive to live by faith. We learn to rejoice that we can come to see with invisible eyes, but we know the answer to that question. Everyone knows it. The farther you travel from the "flesh" that is your own personal embodiment of the human rebellion against God, the more your body, the flesh that is the most glorious work of God's visible creation, becomes real. Sometimes it even becomes raidant, shining with the glory of the risen Lord, but bright with eternity or impossibly opaque with pain, the reality of your own flesh, its immortal *thereness*, only intensifies the more you flee from corruption into the glorious liberty of the children of God. There is no love, then, that is not manifested in the flesh for us. None at all.

But when the Master speaks these words of prodigal love to us, and promises us—all of us, each of us—his body, what do we say to him? This is what I say: "That is what I have been waiting to hear all my life. But I know you, Jesus. I have heard of you, and seen you. How can you do it—give me your flesh and blood, not just to hold, but to eat and drink? Will you be there for me to touch when I am on the mountain alone? Will you be there for me to hold when I walk through the waters? When I am burning with sorrow or falling without end into the abyss that is somehow the very essence of me, will I be able to eat you and drink you then, Lord? How can you promise me that? I have been there, and I cried out for you, and there was no flesh, none, to comfort me, no drink to bring me—not joy or even peace—just simple hope.

"Where were you, Master? When all is going well, and I am able to pray, or trust, or simply believe, when others love me, or when I am simply still in the silence and emptiness that I most truly am, then yes, I can eat your flesh and drink your blood, and I know that I will live. But on the mountain or in the deep waters? In the darkness, in the impenetrable aloneness, in the burning—were you there? Were you feeding me? Why tell me that you will give me flesh to eat and blood to drink if, when I most need to, I cannot touch you, taste you, even guess the human shape of your love?"

And Jesus simply insists: *"My flesh truly is food, and my blood truly is drink, and whoever comes to me will live by the life that I live."* Eternal life, the limitless outpouring that is Father, Son, and Spirit endlessly embracing, saturating, overflowing the bottomlessness of my tiny human flesh: I believe—but where, Lord? How?

In August we celebrate our Lady's going home. We fill our rooms with songs and all the flowers of summer because Mary is entering the new Jerusalem, the heavenly city; because this woman, this female body and human being has been taken absolutely home to God. Even if our minds can scarcely grasp it, our hearts understand. The flesh of our mother, the very roots of our recreated earth, is now so glorified by the Holy Spirit that two bodies, one male and one female, from this tiny planet hidden in the vastness of space are caught up—his by total union with the Word, hers by total union with the Word's grace—into the very center of the Holy Trinity.

Now through Christ's risen presence filling all creation Mary too is present everywhere.

Our whole human flesh, male and female—this fragility, this pain, this joy, this burden, this ecstasy, this beauty, this sorrow, this baptized dust that is the image of infinity—is living forever, the sacrament of life for every creature in the universe. The Master is offering us his solidity—not his "spirit" only, or his mind, or his soul, but his irrefutably human density: his flesh and his blood. He is saying, "If you live my life, if you keep my word, if you only ask me, you will have me. Not an idea of me or a feeling of me or a phantom of me or a dream of me, but *me.* When you reach out in the darkness, I will be there. When you cry out on the mountain, I will be there. When you are in the burning, I will be with you. Not in a way that you can feel at first, but as you keep calling and reaching and burning, you will learn to touch me. More than that: you will eat me, drink me. I will be your food. I will pass through all your organs, through your bones. I will flow in your blood, move through your arms and legs, fill your brain. My flesh will fill even the unfillable recesses of your spirit, and every cell of you will become a cell of me. I will speak my name in your heart."

This is the promise of the flesh and blood of Jesus the Lord, risen and glorified. In the still "flash" of his resurrection I have new words to speak:

> "I am all at once what Christ is, since he was what I am, and
> This Jack, joke, poor potsherd, patch, matchwood, immortal diamond,
> Is immortal diamond."[1]

The Blessed Spirit of God—so transcendent that we cannot have even one idea about him that is literally so—has filled our ordinary, blissful or bored, death-aimed life with the glory of the risen flesh of Jesus. If we have eyes to see, we see him in every face we meet, including our own; or ears to hear, we hear him in both tears and laughter; or mouth to taste, we taste him in every bite of food we eat and every bit of earth we kiss.

"Anyone who eats this bread will live forever." Already, because our flesh and the Master's are one, we are in eternal life. *We* are true flesh: our ragged bodies, vessels of hope and anguish, ashheaps and icons, crazy with loss and speechless with love, already they are transformed so that when we touch one another, we touch—our

[1]Gerard Manley Hopkins, "That Nature Is a Heraclitean Fire and of the Comfort of the Resurrection," ll. 21-24.

Lord and our God. How can it be? Does it matter how, finally? It is: taste, touch, and see. That is the only necessity—that we not go away, shaking our heads, grumbling over the hard words, smug that even the Master disappointed us. We only need to keep coming to the table, day after day after day until the end, when we will see with our own eyes Jesus's flesh in our own. In simplicity we answer the insistence of Jesus with our own insistence: "Give it to me, your flesh and your blood. I want it. I can't live without it."

If we keep coming and wanting and asking, then even before our eyes are clear enough to see the full glory of our own flesh, we will find that the Master has laid his table for us by every tree, in the middle of every moment, in the silent core of every heart. Jesus has spread out his banquet of love in my brother's flesh, in my sister's, in my own. "Come," he says, and so I will eat and drink, and I will live forever.

MAKING CONNECTIONS

Our skin seems to us like a barrier for two reasons. Because we are animals, we move about more or less in possession of our own life-support systems. Because we are human animals, we know that there is about us something unique, incommunicable. We feel our distinctness from every other creature. Because I am uniquely I, I assume that my being stops at the edge of my skin: "I" am here. Everything else is where I am not.

Of course even biologically this is only a partial truth. My skin is not a wall, but a membrane, a marvelously complex organ of communication and exchange. On this splendid summer day as I sit in the sun, the whole earth, all of the cosmos, sends messages to me through my skin. The earth speaks to me in green syllables of grass. The soft air cleanses and warms my heart as well as my body. The earth's star pours its bright energies, the energies of the entire galaxy, down upon me. The world flows into me, and I into it, but so quietly that I recognize that I am immersed in the stream of the universe no more than a cod swimming nonchalantly in the depths of the ocean is aware of the water moving through him as he moves through it.

One simple element in the story of two healings in the fifth chapter of Mark's Gospel reveals the way the seemingly random linkages of our flesh become the hinges on which our salvation hangs. The Gospel draws a sharp contrast between the two people in need of healing – the daughter of Jairus and the hemorrhaging woman. One is at least a mature woman, the other a little girl. The faith of one carries her to Jesus through all manner of obstacles after she has been stripped of everything she hoped in. The other dies suddenly, and Jesus the Master is brought to her by the faith of others. One gropes through a crowd to touch Jesus, while the other rests in the passivity of death as Jesus reaches out to her. But one thing ties them together: the little girl is twelve years old, the same age as the older woman's hemorrhage.

Did that little girl in the rest of her life on earth ever come to know that one of the reasons she was born was to become sick and suddenly to die, to draw Jesus to her through the grief of her father so that the Master might pass by within touching distance of the woman with the hemorrhage, whose disease began the same year the little girl was born? Did that healed woman ever realize that God began to plan to make her whole again at the very moment that he allowed her to experience her affliction? A coincidence? What is a coincidence but a connection we haven't yet learned to understand?

Unconsciously we read the Gospels with a kind of skepticism. We read about the victories of Jesus, and we wonder if there were also failures. What about those who were not healed, the people of his home town, for example? Even if we try hard not to be skeptical, we look carefully to discover the technique of faith. What does the hemorrhaging woman do, what does Jairus do, that enables the Lord to heal? We trust much less in the power of his love than we do in the power of our minds to put the pieces of life together in such a way that the Master will be forced to do what we want.

Yet these two stories are not tales of human success. They are simply revelations of the healing that is available to everyone. The real healing is that Jesus walked into the lives of these people. Because he walked in, physical healings took place, but the great healing is the gift of his presence, the living experience of his love that he makes available wherever he goes. What of all the others—suspicious Nazarenes, by-standers, people pushing at him, perhaps thinking of him as just another wandering magician? Somehow, their lives too were blessed by his presence so that, afterwards, they never forgot how their hearts beat or how they smelled joy in the air the day that he passed by.

The mystery of pain and sorrow in human life is nearly infinite. True, God did not make human death. Humans made it out of the suicide that is sin. Yet what are to make of that decision for death and of God's decision to let the world go on, infected by death, until it became saturated with pain, like once-new wool steeped in scarlet dye? The pain is inescapable. We all experience enormous losses. Even if we manage to evade catastrophe or destitution and to steel ourselves against the certainty of death, no one can escape loss when each of us swims through a universe that never stops flowing, that brings together only to separate again, that steeps us in pain to the very degree to which we open ourselves to its loveliness. And more powerful in many ways than our own suffering is the agony of others, over which we have even less control and the end of which we shall so certainly never see until our amazed eyes stroke their risen bodies and know what we ourselves look like from the beauty of their transfigured faces.

Suddenly, I am thinking of bread baking and of Mary, making connections about connections. A friend once told me how—half-crazy with loneliness, cut off from his grim past in Europe, an alien in Canada, despairing of a future that promised him nothing but what he'd already tried to flee—he had walked out onto a bridge intending to jump to his death. Then, as he stood by the rail, something penetrated his isolation: not God, not his family, not his true worth, but simply the smell of bread baking. On the other side of the river there was a huge bread factory, and the smell of it—not like a country oven, but not at all like the other smells of the city either—made my friend realize that there was one simple, ordinary thing that he did not, after all, want to lose. For one crucial moment the reality of bread was more significant than the enormity of his pain. The smell of bread saved his life.

I don't think it matters whether or not my friend unconsciously remembered his mother's tenderness or perhaps his grandmother's, at the very moment he seemed most alone. Nor is it important to know if the smell of bread baking roused in him some deeply hidden memory of the Eucharist. God was in that smell just as surely as if his Son had bent over that factory and had spoken the words of consecration over the whole night's baking. In fact, I think that that is what had already happened, and that is the reason I am thinking of the Mother of Jesus.

This is the Gospel: one ordinary day, perhaps in early spring but in any case a day not in mythic time or metahistorical time or in symbolic time, but at a certain moment in the earth's revolution around the sun, God spoke to a young woman and touched her body, and his eternal Word became flesh. And on another day, this one certainly in spring, but just as commonplace as the other, the Son of that woman gathered his own crucified flesh into his inmost grip and plunged it totally into the Father. In that instant—though his friends came to know it only later, when they experienced it in their own bodies—all matter was saturated with immortal light, and human flesh became the glory of God made visible. And when the Mother of Jesus fell asleep in death, he touched her body with his glory and made her for all time the fragrance of his joy – the sweet odor of bread rising and baking throughout the whole universe.

The Good News is that Jesus, God's Son, our Master and Lord, has walked through creation, healing and transforming it. But he has not come and gone. He has come and has stayed. Now and again I have dreams of flying. My body, just as solid as ever, becomes lighter than air, as agile as an angel. Often as I zoom and swoop or simply hover in a holding pattern the thought occurs to me that I'm only dreaming, but at once I reject the idea simply because it is so apparent that such freedom is the state of my true being.

Sometimes faith seems like flying, the true grace that we say it is. My mind, my emotions, my heart grow still enough for me truly to taste and smell and touch and see and hear, and I find that the Master has given me the living knowledge of his presence so that the God whom no mouth can taste, no nose smell, no hand touch, no eye see, no ear hear is flowing through me more palpably than my blood. At such times I am not dancing on air. My agility is so inward that the only way you might see it would be to recognize that my face had assumed its own true shape – and that my eyes had become free enough to see the true shape of yours. There is no dancing on air: only the marvelous sense of having my feet at last on truly solid ground as skillful hands unwrap from me the rotten strips of cloth that I had thought for so long were the skin of my soul.

If the Master has walked in and lifted us out of death, then why are we still in the process of rising? Why do some people spend thirty years on the cross or fifty in the tomb? Who knows? Why does it take so long – almost 2000 years now – to make all the connections? I don't know. What I know is that the connections are being made, in me, in those I live with and touch, in the entire world. Bones reconnected, sinews reattached, nerves and muscles restrung, flesh restored, faces reawakened, hearts made new: and the whole universe is ringing with the alleluia that this Easter people is learning to sing with a single voice. What I know is that Jesus has brought life into my life. He is the beauty of God, the face of the Father made visible. He is the compassion of God, the love of the Father made touchable, made as close as human flesh. He is the connection that is life without end. In him all alienations are ending in reconciliation, and all dead-ends are being turned into passages of communion. Heaven and earth are already full of his glory.

An author of the second century wrote: "Happy are they who have put all their trust in the cross and have plunged into the water of life."

Jesus the Master has passed through our pain. He has passed through all our losses. He has passed through our death, and now he calls us to plunge into the river of life into which his death has transformed all of creation – and every human heart. He has made that plunge very simple: sometimes we only have to reach out our hands to touch him; sometimes we need to call out to him, "Come, Lord. My daughter, my son, my sister, my brother, my beloved is dying." But he will always come because he loves us and because he wants to bring us the joy of his presence, the gift of his life.

When the Master feels the power of that life going forth from him in the midst of that noisy, jostling crowd, he stops, turns his face, and his eyes search out the one who touched him. She comes forward, healed but still frightened, and he says to her, though before she touched him she was no longer young, "Daughter." She looks at his face, and her fear goes. Jesus has done for her what he came to do: he has shown her the face of tenderness, the face of the Father. From that day on the skin of that woman's face shines with the glory shining so ordinarily on the face of Jesus, and every event in her life, every encounter, is a coincidence of love.

THE PRAYER OF FAITH

Once, in the early days of charismatic prayer meetings, I happened to open my eyes and glance over at someone who had begun to pray aloud. We had worked together often in my first two summers at Madonna House, but we hadn't often been stationed in the same place since then. Still, I think we knew each other well, as members of big families do if they pay attention at all to their brothers and sisters. My Madonna House brother read a long psalm—Psalm 107, I recall—and then began to thank and praise the Lord in his own words for his goodness and his love. As he prayed, his face began to shine—not like the sun, but just like his own true face as it was when the Master's eyes were looking at it. I had never seen my brother's face before that because I had never heard, perhaps never listened, to his heart praying.

Since then, I've known that, if I wanted, Jesus would always let me see the true faces of my brothers and my sisters if I listened deeply to the prayer of their hearts. Sometimes it seems easy. Love or holiness or poverty or suffering opens the door, and you walk right in, and you see the face that the Master sees. Sometimes he shows it to you when the friend he brings you is in great need, and you step down with him into a wound that he is making into a well of light. For many you must listen patiently and with great care before the daily face begins to shine with the light of Nazareth. For some, of course—those who have set their minds and hearts against the Gospel or the way you live it, beloved ones who have left and gone far away, and especially those whom you yourself have betrayed—your own heart has to break and shatter if you want to journey very deep down to the new day where you and they can stand together in the sun that is the Master himself, risen from the dead.

Sometimes it seems easy to see another's true face, but it is never easy because to see truly, you must forget yourself and let the Master show you that love is infinitely deep. You could drown in such depths; some have. Yet words like "easy" and "hard" and even risks like drowning lose their power when you find the mustard seed of faith within you, and understand that the Master himself has put it there. No one can take it from you, and if you put into his hands its rooting and its growth, you will find the Spirit making it a prayer of stillness enabling you to hear another's heart and see another's face, and your own, and his. Let us watch and listen as the Master shows us how it happened once.

> Jesus withdrew to the region of Tyre and Sidon. Then out came a Canaanite woman from that district and started shouting, "Lord, Son of David, have mercy on me! My daughter is severely possessed by a demon!" But he did not answer her a word.
>
> Then his disciples went and pleaded with him. "Send her away," they said, "because she keeps crying out after us." Jesus replied, "I was sent only to the lost sheep of the house of Israel."
>
> But the woman came up and knelt before him. "Lord," she said, "help me!"
>
> He answered, "It is not fair to take the children's bread and throw it to the dogs."
>
> "Yes, Lord." she said, "but even the dogs eat the crumbs that fall from their master's table."
>
> Then Jesus answered and said to her, "Woman, great is your faith! Let it be done to you as you desire." And her daughter was healed at that very moment (Mt 15:21-28; cf. Mk 7:24-30).

Who knows what this story, or any passage of Scripture, means except God? Only God knows, and the Master he has sent us, and the Holy Spirit who will remind us how he spoke and will teach us to understand him. Only those humble and trusting enough to be still, to listen, to hear, and to obey will understand. This story speaks of the mysteries of faith and prayer, of listening and hearing. It tells of a woman empowered to hear the Word of God. It tells of the Word of God listening two people, not one, into new life.

Here we see a woman begin with a frenzy for her daughter's healing and end in meeting the Master of her heart. Here we see a Canaanite, a pagan, let the extraordinarily harsh words of the Master uncover the true depth of her heart, where he becomes her servant. This is what the Word of God – in Scripture, in all the seasons and passages of our lives, in all those we meet – is meant to do to us and for us. This story discloses the meaning of the prayer of faith. It is not a lesson plan that teaches the proper techniques of Christian prayer, but if we have ears to hear, and an open heart, it shows us how we can come to the Master of our life, who is our Savior and the world's.

Like many of our own stories of faith and prayer, this one springs forth from pain. A mother is at her wit's end because her daughter is so severely vexed by a demon. Somehow, she hears that Jesus has come nearby. Perhaps she even leaves her native place and goes into the territory of the Jews to look for a healer. This "Canaanite," a member of the primordial enemies of Israel and Israel's God, knows how to address the healer she finds: "Lord, Son of David!" She knows what to ask him, as the whole Church has asked him every day since his resurrection: "*Kyrie, eleison*": "Lord, have mercy!" He answers nothing.

This Canaanite mother continues, literally, to make a scene. The Gospel says that she was "shouting" or "crying out." Whatever she is doing — shrieking, sobbing, screaming, grabbing the disciples' hands, clutching at their clothes, tearing her own, stumbling and thrashing like a wounded beast — it is more than enough to drive the disciples to intercede for her with the Master. He calmly, even coolly reminds them that Israel is his flock. Jesus knows his vocation and means to accomplish it.

But the mother knows too what she wants, and she means to get it. She comes right up to this one whom she has called "Lord," and kneels, or as the Greek of the Gospel plainly implies, falls prostrate before him. Now a suppliant, a worshiper, she asks her Lord for help. She is no longer making a scene. She has entered a relationship. She has begun a conversation.

But is she still lying with her face in the dust? Has she yet looked at this Master whose title and power she knows, but whose name she has not spoken? However that may be, Jesus uses what is probably a folk proverb to get her full attention, not just any proverb, but one so mocking in this context, one that denies so cuttingly any obligation, responsibility, interest, not to speak of mercy, that it seems a racist line drawn in the air between them.

Now this woman is surely looking at Jesus. She is no longer screaming and shrieking, grabbing clothes, clutching at God. She is no longer possessed by her daughter's pain. She is no longer out of her wits, but in full possession of them. She is a woman, and as smart as she is needy. This man, who is still Lord, probably all the more so in the tough authority of his self-possession, has something she wants, and she still means to get it. This woman has her wits about her now, and she uses them to top the Master's proverb with a saying of her own. But she wins the day not with cleverness, but with clear-hearted acceptance of her own littleness. She doesn't know the Master's plan or her people's place in it. She doesn't know much about his bread, either, except that it comes from heaven, but she does know that just a crumb will satisfy her. She doesn't even ask for it. She simply tells this man she's looking at with total clarity now that she knows he can give what she's asking for if he wants.

Jesus corrects her one last time — with praise. "Woman!" A cloud of silence has fallen around this woman and this man. They are alone together, these two, still Jew and Canaanite, Lord and suppliant, Middle-eastern man and Middle-eastern woman, but now they are also Master and disciple, and therefore this man speaking to this woman. They are not exactly equals, but they are two persons together, talking intimately. You might call them friends.

"Great is your faith!" Jesus shows the woman what he has found in her. He shows her that as he led her from frenzy to stillness, from instinctive hunger for supernatural help to a living bond of trust with him, so she persisted, opened herself, listened, and followed him to a place of meeting, where two loves could become one to heal her daughter — or the world. The Master might have told her, "Blessed is she who is not scandalized by me!" In teaching her how to pray, he revealed to her the true depth of her own life and the treasure that the Father himself put there: "No one can come to me unless the Father enable him" (Jn 6:65). This treasure no one can take from her, for it raises the center of her spirit where it dwells into the Kingdom, where no thief can break in and steal, or moth consume, or time decay. Both the woman of faith and her daughter were healed at that moment.

But why does this journey of faith and to faith, this passage into true prayer of the heart take so long? We can't know, precisely, any more than we can know, precisely, why the journey is so painful. We do know something, however. We know that the Master can hasten the time when he finds someone as steadfast and as responsive as the Canaanite woman. We know that he does not want to heal our symptoms until he cures the blindness of our souls and gives us eyes to see and know him as he is — the Lord and the servant of our life.

By silence, by hard answers, by challenging questions, the Master draws us to himself. "Keep coming," he says, because he wants to draw us into the true place of meeting, where we recognize our blindness and have nowhere else to go for sight except to him, who wants to show us his face, the face of the Lover of every woman and man he has made and redeemed with his Father and the Holy Spirit. And when we get there at last, he says, "I've been waiting for you." He is waiting for us, but not passively. He waits as he draws us, draws us into the center of our being and his.

We are distracted by so many things, especially by pain – our own anguish, the miseries of the world, the suffering of those we love. Yet Christ the risen Master is in our midst – in our very midst; in the depth of our hearts – feeding us with the Father's love, filling us with the power of his life. In helplessness we scurry around, make plans, enlist in causes, write books. We read, we go to doctors and priests, we try spiritual programs, we seek love everywhere. We seem to do everything but be still, and look, and listen.

Because Jesus cares so much for us and knows our dreadful powerlessness, he became powerlessness itself for us. He gave everything and now he does everything to focus our attention. He wants us to enlist him in our cause. He wants to give us the miracle of faith so that the scattered flock can come together at last and build its house on the rock of his love. The Master wants us to be one, empowered by his omnipotent word to love one another as he loves us.

He says to us, "Come to me all you who are weary and heavily laden, and I will give you rest. Take my yoke upon you, and learn from me, for I am meek and humble of heart, and you will find rest for your souls. For my yoke is easy, and my burden is light," (Mt 11:28-30). But he is also saying, "*You* come to *me*, not some shadow you to some shadow of me. *You* come to *me.* Keep coming. Don't give up. You're getting there. It's worth it."

Of course it's worth it. Jesus Christ truly is the Master of life. He truly is the Son of God, God made flesh, forgiveness of our sins, eternal life out of death, desire of our hearts, comfort and peace and exaltation of the poor. To speak to him face to face and heart to heart is already the Kingdom. To let his light break forth in us is to bring his light to every face we meet, to every name in our hearts, to every unknown child of God he has made our sister or brother. The prayer of faith gives his resurrection to the world.

KINGDOM, POWER, AND GLORY

Jesus was on his way to Jerusalem and death. He had "set his face" toward the city, as Luke puts it (Lk 9:52). He was "leading the way," as Mark writes (Mk 10:32), while his disciples followed in astonishment—at his boldness? at his eagerness?—and the rest of the crowd buzzed along in fear. The air must have been loud with questions, shouted and unspoken. The Master took the Twelve aside and told them what would happen to him—betrayal, condemnation, mockery, abuse, flogging, execution, and resurrection.

The Twelve were never at their best when Jesus warned them about his death and prepared them for his resurrection. Even in John's Gospel, in the comparatively serene setting of the Last Discourse, they are filled with nagging questions and rumble with argument. Who can blame them, really? Jesus had become everything for them, after all, and when Peter had pointed that out to him, Jesus had been quick to promise them everything, including persecutions (Mk 10:28-29). Still, James and John seem to respond to the Master's sharing of his deepest heart with a self-centered disregard that rings across the centuries like a slap in the face:

> "Master," they said, "we want you to do for us whatever we ask."
> "What do you want me to do for you?" he asked.
> They replied, "Let one of us sit at your right and the other at the left in your glory" (Mk 10:35-37).

However, even leaving aside Matthew's version of this story, in which the mother of James and John kneels or prostrates herself before Jesus and then asks him a favor (Mt 20:20 ff.), we might listen more carefully to Zebedee's sons' request and the Master's answer. They seem to be asking for status and power, but isn't it possible that they are instead confidently asking for intimacy? Wasn't it perhaps because they *loved* Jesus that they wanted to be right next to him forever? Of course they wanted to be princes or viceroys, but hadn't the Master promised thrones to the Twelve? Why shouldn't theirs be as close to his as possible?

Jesus the Master caught all of this. He saw very clearly that "the sons of thunder" were young and full of fire, that they were drawn to him because they believed that, somehow, he was the King, and they wanted to reign with him in his Kingdom. He knew too that they loved him and wanted to be near him. But he had to teach them more: they didn't know what they were asking. "Can you drink my cup or be baptized with the baptism I am baptized with?" They would have understood the "cup." The saying is similar to our question, "Can you eat what's on my plate?" or "Can you take what I am going to take?" James and John would have understood that the cup of the Master would be bitter to drain, but they couldn't have grasped the depth of his baptism. They would have known what baptism was. John the Baptist had baptized many with his baptism of repentance. They would have heard something about John's baptism of Jesus, and they must have guessed that it implied for the Master himself some total immersion in the Father's will. Maybe they also sensed that Jesus was speaking about the sacrificial aspect of his own suffering and death, but they clearly didn't realize the link between that and his glory. In eager ignorance they said, "Yes, we can do what you will do."

The Master's response points directly to the reality that links cup, baptism, and throne—the will of the Father. This is the link that James and John have missed. Yes, they will drink Christ's cup and share his baptism, but the depth of the cup and the center of the baptism is total abandonment to the Father. He alone has made Jesus Master and Christ; he alone will confer glory, kingship, and power on him through the humiliation of the cross; he alone knows who belongs where in the Kingdom his Son is establishing through his humble submission.

Then, not just because the pushy two have provoked jealousy in the other ten, but because the Master loves them all and wants them to understand how twelve—or a thousand or 750 million or five billion—can be one, he gathers his friends together and reveals to them the secret of the glorified life.

> You know that those who are regarded as rulers of the Gentiles lord it over them, and their high officials make their power felt. Not so among you. Instead, whoever wants to become great among you must be your servant, and whoever wants to be first must be slave of

> all. For even the Son of Man did not come to be served, but to serve, and to give his life as ransom for many (Mk 10:41-45).

In the Kingdom, in the *real* world, power flows from humble, serving, sacrificial love.

Christians are still grappling with this revelation. We practice it with great difficulty. Do non-Christians look at the Church, the sacrament of the Kingdom on earth and say, "See how differently they run things from the way we do! Look at the humility of those Christians before one another!" We need to listen to what the Master has taught us about authority and power in the Kingdom.

In the first place, Christ clearly says that not everyone "among us" is called to be "great," but only those who want to serve. Only the one who wants to be "the slave of all" is called to be "first." In a supremely status-conscious culture, which prizes individual freedom and power, this teaching comes as a liberation as well as a challenge. Not everyone has to be the least: only the one who wants to be first. If I don't want to be everyone's slave, then I don't have to; if I want a little greatness, then I can try serving two or three. But if I don't want to surrender my "personality" or my "space" or my "creativity," I don't have to in order to be loved by God. I will, however, have to be humble before those courageous enough to choose to serve me.

Secondly, the Master tells us that servanthood is, in the strictest meaning of the word, a mystery because it is unbreakably bound to his own choice to serve and to lay down his life "as a ransom." Most of us have never thought of servanthood as a mystery. In North America "serving" and "service"—within unspoken but definite limits—have entered the culture's lifeblood as well as its jargon, mellowing capitalism, blurring class distinctions, even masking the painful necessity of a military establishment. Where else are the armed forces called "the Service"? But actually to be a servant? That is nearly unthinkable—except for the desperate. Servants lack status and, moreover, the control over their lives needed to build a flattering image out of power, money, or possessions. Others pull their strings. From the time they get up until the time they go to bed others' wishes are their commands. Their masters and mistresses know how to make them feel the authority they are under. Even if, Jeeves-like, servants contrive to turn a household hierarchy on its head, they are still persons who have put their own selves aside to be at the disposal of others. What most cultures have taken for granted and what North America finds morally and socially irresponsible, Jesus the Master makes a mystery. He does not hold on to his eternal equality with God, but shows that, in human life, his infinite love for the Father becomes infinitely humble service "for many" – for as many as will accept it. The Master puts himself aside for us.

Most find the mystery of servanthood magnificent in Jesus, and perhaps most Christians at least recognize in it a personal "ideal"; but many Christians also tend to think it hopelessly romantic or even preposterous as the basic "rule" of social action. Many very smart people find it far easier to imagine the "withering away of the state" than a humble Pope or priest or bank president. Many very good Catholics believe, some passionately, that the powerlessness of such a profound and intimate self-disarmament is spiritual regression that runs directly counter to the way God himself empowers us to live freely in Christ. Then what are they – or we, all of us – to make of the Master's insistence that in the Kingdom the "great" are those who have become "slaves of all"?

Is it religious rhetoric? Is it simply Christ's way of saying what other wise men have said, that littleness holds a special power? Is it opium, a pleasant escape that leads to a deadly addiction – a kind of suicide? And even if this "slavery" is true as an "ideal," oughtn't we update it in light of the abuses that such imagery must have contributed to – not only Christian slavemasters and autocratic fathers, but priest-ridden peasants and psychically abused religious, the whole shadowside of Christian life that we ignore at the risk of losing sight of the risen Christ in our midst? That he offers us the liberating power of the Father's love we all agree. But what is the secret of his glory?

"If anyone wishes to come after me, he must deny himself and take up his cross and follow me. For whoever wants to save his life will lose it, but whoever loses his life for me and the gospel will save it" (Mk 8:34-35). How can we be ashamed of the language of the cross when neither the Master nor his disciples were ashamed? "Slave" is a harsh and ugly word. Perhaps the reality of unchosen bondage is even harsher and uglier now than it was in the early first century. If so, it is because the Master "scorned the shame" of the cross (Heb 12:2), and by freely choosing to become the slave of all, transformed suffering and death itself into sacraments of life. Coercing others to enlarge the kingdom of my self is especially loathsome after centuries of the Gospel life, lived however imperfectly by countless millions of women and men, have showed that suffering with and for the crucified Master (and all his friends) brings freedom and peace, not oppression and despair. The "slavery" that Christ spoke of and lived leads to the communion of saints on earth as well as in eternity because it is not a yielding to blind Fate, but an intimate sharing of Christ's own trust in the Father's love. James and John wanted to be fully united with the Master in his glory, and he showed them how to wash the feet of others.

* * *

I am sitting here in Combermere on a flawless summer day in ordinary time. Is this a poustinia or an oasis? The sky is a canopy of blue over a green world, whose leaves and grasses are rippling in a light wind. I can hear a few cars in the distance, but no human voices. Most of the birds are resting. A few sing little songs in the trees. You would know what it means to call something smooth as silk if you could see the river running full without a sound. It is still cool, but warm enough to swim in.

If I turned on a radio, this serene country day would find its anguished twentieth-century voice at once. Wars and rumors of wars, terrorists' bombs and hijackings, woes of children, woes of farmers, woes of the "great" and woes of the unknown, arguments of partisans and cries of the helpless everywhere – the "news," the bitter bread our groaning world bakes for us daily, would feed me all the pain the sweet summer air does not let me see or smell. But I don't need to turn on the radio. My mind is tuning me in quite nicely, thank you. It is saying, "Are you crazy? Why are you writing these foolish words about Jesus and washing feet? If they didn't believe him, why would they believe you? Besides, even if a few did believe you, think of the billions of words spoken and written since he spoke and acted – and became a ransom. Don't you know that everyone, even believers, has a stake in power – powerful and powerless alike? After centuries of explanation and interpretation, do you think anyone wants to let *you* have the final word? Talk about power! And even more to the point, just what are your credentials. . . ?"

* * *

Credentials: yes, that's what we were talking about, the credentials of power; or rather, that is what Jesus, James, and John were talking about before I interrupted them with ironies of sun and starvation, casuistry and birdsongs. Yet the Master knows what irony is. Hasn't he just been showing his skill in the use of it – great one and servant, first and slave, glorious King and ransom for many? And isn't his whole Gospel – not merely this teaching about power, but the entire Good News – based on the irony of the smallest thing, the seed of greatest tininess and most apparent insignificance, that becomes the tree where all creation comes to rest?

With all his skill the Master is proclaiming the irony of love. Jesus, like more recent revolutionaries, urges deeds, not words: "Not everyone who says to me, 'Lord, Lord,' will enter the Kingdom of heaven, but the one who does the will of my Father in heaven" (Mt 7:21). "Rather, blessed are they who hear the word of God and keep it" (Lk 11:28). "'You should have put my money on deposit with the bankers so that when I returned, I would have received it back with interest'" (Mt 25:27). But unlike lesser revolutionaries, Jesus knows what power truly is. The "money" of God that must be spent, the word of God that must be lived, the will of the Father that is the key to the Kingdom and to each one's place in it is, in the final irony of his unlimited simplicity, love:

> You have heard that it was said, "Love your neighbor and hate your enemy." But I tell you, Love your enemies and pray for those who persecute you, that you may be sons of your Father in heaven. He makes his sun rise on the evil and the good, and sends rain on the righteous and the unrighteous. If you love those who love you, what reward will you get? Are not even the tax collectors doing that? And if you greet only your brothers, what are you doing more than others? Do not even pagans do that? Be perfect, therefore, as your heavenly Father is perfect (Mt 5:43-48).
>
> A new commandment I give you: love one another as I have loved you (Jn 13:34).

In the immeasurable depth of the Master's baptism God's very being transforms all things. Here is the empowerment of the powerless, the homecoming of the dispossessed, liberty to captives, good news to the poor: what is impossible to men is possible for God. The suffering of the weak and the broken, in the furnace of Christ's love and by the grace of his cross, becomes the gold of mercy; and even the rich can learn to pass through the needle's eye of love into the Kingdom of peace. God himself is sleeplessly at our disposal, knocking on our doors, waiting patiently to bring us the banquet of love.

The words of the Eucharist that the Church offers every day from the rising of the sun to its setting say it all: "This is my body . . . for you." "Given for you," we say, or "broken for you," or "given up for you," but however we say it, the reality of the Master's gift lies with infinite simplicity on the altar. He became flesh for us. He became sin for us. He became glory for us. He becomes food for us. If we take and eat this bread of the divine humility, and drink from the cup of the Servant "who was rich, yet for our sakes became poor, so that through his poverty we might become rich" (2 Cor 8:9), we are plunged into the power that made the first light, and now has made all things subject to him. By that same power he forever offers himself—for us. Now, if we want, we can too become perfect subjects of Love himself.

He will teach us. He will show us how to spell love with our lives. He will give us many, a few, at least someone to serve. He will lead us deep within ourselves, to the place of true silence where the Father has already made his home in us, and the communion of saints has already begun. We will be with the Master forever as friends.

WATCH!

"Watch!" the Master commands when he speaks of his coming (Mt 24:42). "Watch!" he urges in the parable of the wise and foolish virgins (Mt 24:1-13). "Watch!" he insists: he is a bridegroom who comes like a thief in the night (Lk 12:39; Rev 3:3). "Watch, therefore, for you do not know when the master of the house will come — in the evening, or at midnight, or at cockcrow, or in the morning — lest he come suddenly and find you asleep. And what I say to you I say to all: 'Watch!'" (Mk 13:35-37).

Watching: it means looking and listening in such a way that you are prepared to meet the Master when he comes. It means learning to read the "signs of the times" so that your heart is ready to greet the Bridegroom. Yet it is not merely political and cosmic events we Christians must learn to read. "Be attentive!" the Byzantine liturgy directs — that you may discern the Lord's presence in the Gospel and in the Eucharist. And the Master himself says, "I was hungry, and you fed me..." (Mt 25:35).

The Master will come, yes, with all his angels in the glory of his Father, but he comes now too. "Behold, I stand at the door and knock. If anyone hears my voice and opens the door, I will come in to him and sup with him, and he with me" (Rev 3:20). He comes so silently in the poor that even the blessed minister to him in ignorance. Surely, though, his promise that he will come in and "sup" with us — to restore to us the original intimacy of the "cool of the evening" — invites us, now, to enter a personal, conscious communion in love with him. Surely Thomas Traherne was right: "We need only have an open eye for our hearts to be ravished like the cherubim."

Jesus told us as much himself when he said, "Blessed are the pure of heart, for they shall see God" (Mt 5:8). It is the pure of heart who see with an open eye, whose hearts are ravished even now by the face of the risen Master, who live in the glory of the Holy Trinity and know, beginning even here, the perfect joy that St. Francis knew and that pierced Mary's heart as she cried out, "Rabboni!" (Jn 20:16). Such a heart is the heart of a child, but it is also the heart of a hunter, a hunter for the presence of God made flesh.

Listen to José Ortega y Gasset on the way a hunter watches:

> He does not look tranquilly in one determined direction, sure beforehand that the game will pass in front of him. The hunter knows that he does not know what is going to happen, and this is one of the greatest attractions of his occupation. Thus he needs to prepare an attention of a different and superior style – an attention which does not consist in riveting itself on the presumed but consists precisely in not presuming anything and avoiding inattentiveness. It is a "universal" attention, which does not inscribe itself on any point and tries to be on all points. There is a magnificent term for this, one that still conserves all its zest of vivacity and imminence: alertness. The hunter is the alert man.[1]

Our "game" is God, and the truly alert are those who presume nothing and delight in the way in which their being stretches out to touch all that is around them. They expect the unexpected. They are empty of everything but silence. They know that what they seek is, like other game, "scarce," rare. It presents itself when it chooses: "it is a flash of opportunity the hunter must take advantage of."[2] Thus in hunters for God the "passion" of receiving has become wholly active as all they are leans toward the meeting that is their life. They become conscious of the air itself so that at its slightest movement they may, as St. John of the Cross has said, "leap into the abyss to seize their prey."

Yet despite God's elusiveness, if we are those who truly watch, each moment becomes an epiphany. St. Augustine has written this about the discovery of God:

> Some people, in order to discover God, read books. But there is a great book: the very appearance of created things. Look above you! Look below you! Note it; read it. God, whom you want to discover, never wrote that book with ink; instead he set before your eyes the things that he had made. Can you ask for a louder voice than that? Why, heaven and earth shout to you: "God made me!"[3]

---

[1]*Meditations on Hunting*, trans. (New York: Charles Scribner's Sons, 1972).

[2]Ibid.

[3]*Sermo CXXVI*, 6, from *Nova Patrum Bibliotheca: Sermones CCII* (Sancti Augustini), ed. Angelo Cardinal Mai, Rome, 1852. See Hugh Pope, *St. Augustine of Hippo* (New York: Image Books, 1961), pp.227, 392-3, 398.

Each thing says, "God," and our ears hear their voice, and the Word of his silence speaks to us. Each thing reflects the perfect Image of God, and our eyes see our Master's glory in all that is small and ordinary. The world becomes a simple banquet for us to share with him.

A still more marvelous thing happens. As our hearts begin to learn the alertness of the hunter of God, the human landscape surrounding us shifts, changes, and suddenly becomes clear. Our old categories—strangers, acquaintances, friends, enemies, relatives, lovers—dissolve. We are no longer riveted on the presumed, and so we are open to the unexpected joy: as each face we meet becomes truly itself, the radiance of Christ himself appears on each. Each man and woman becomes who he or she truly is, and in that very instant we find ourselves looking upon the one Image of the Father. The features that were loved or feared, the voices that were dear or despised, the presences that were shunned or welcomed—all are caught up now in a single Presence. We have sought him, and at last we have let him find us.

Love has sought us, and at last we have let our hearts become simple enough for Love. St. Thomas Aquinas has written, *Ubi amor, ibi oculus*: "Where love is, there is the eye."[4] That little saying holds the deep core of the mystery of watching. For let us speak the whole truth: even when the world begins to reveal the beauty of the Father; even when the face of Jesus the Master begins to shine on us in the faces that we meet, the world made by sin and the flesh twisted by rebellion do not disappear. Often, in fact, they become grosser and more disfigured as the clear presence of the Lord reveals the horror of all that has been misshaped by the rejection of his love.

Where love is, there is the eye. Love reveals Love. In the film made about Mother Teresa's work in Calcutta with the dying and the abandoned, "Something Beautiful for God," one scene shows Mother Teresa and Malcolm Muggeridge walking through a nursery filled with bony, hollow-eyed babies. Horrified, Muggeridge points to the most wizened of all, too frail even to cry, and asks, "What about that one? Will she make it?" Mother Teresa picks her up, and as the camera watches her watching that struggling little face, suddenly her own face becomes all eye, indescribably tender, filled with passionate, joyful strength. "Oh yes!" she says. "She has so much life in her!"

---

[1]*De Dilectione Dei*, 14; see Pope, p. 398.

One's mind begins to cry out in protest, as perhaps Muggeridge's did, but one's inner heart knows that Mother Teresa is right. She has looked and watched, and she has *seen*. As she held and watched this child, who could doubt that she saw Christ, the Master of life?

It is just here that we recognize why we resist learning to watch, to learn alertness, to become hunters of God. Apparent death is all about us, not only in faraway places, in starving children and bomb-torn bodies, but in the terror of our own poor, in the hopelessness of our own friends. We fear their hunger and their need. We fear the demands their nakedness makes on us. We fear that if we let ourselves see them, we will become like them, stripped of illusion and comfort, vulnerable to the whole universe. If we let ourselves become hunters of God, won't we become the hunted, never secure, always seeking, knowing nothing, completely poor, lonely and adrift in an overcrowded boat on a shoreless sea? How can we live with unveiled eyes?

The Master does not really explain it to us. Still less does he force us to watch for him. He only tells us that, if we want, we can be as poor as he is – and as free. He simply invites us to look, to be pierced with his death – and to be filled with the joy of his new life. If we step into the country of his love, we move beyond all illusory frontiers. We will die to the safety of sleep, and awake to an endless vigil of love.

The Master compels us in nothing, but promises us everything. He is coming now, today. If we seek, we shall find. If we stand in the clear, risky air of the Father's world, and let everything and each person come alive for us, we shall live too. If we watch until our whole being becomes a single eye, a center of absolute yearning, then we shall see what we were made to see: things as they truly are. In the ordinary time forged by the Son's gift of love to the Father and to us the Holy Spirit will give us his own eyes to see this new world, remade by the One who has "leaped across our hills" and gazed in secret behind our lattices (Sg 2:8-9). The dawning of his face is our resurrection as we capture him who has already captured us – and look into the eyes of the One who has watched every person, every creature, back to life.

CLOWNING

Well of course she cried, you clowns!
Her eyes had never looked on such a day:
The sun tossed into the midsummer sky
A crystal ball hanging by unseen strings
Its magic revealing the earth's full shape,
Flat but gently sloping inward
Ten trillion stalks of wheat neatly rowed,
Nodding silent heads at the goings-on,
From the far-circle where the blue big-top ended
Right on down to the center ring, the village
That had shed its everyday make-believe
Flung aside its worn routine mask
To show itself a show
A carnival of carousel and ferris-wheel
A festival of booths and jubilee
And smack between leftover banks and stores
A parade:
A centennial dance of majorettes and vets
Where horns and bag-pipes, high school drums and tubas
Wove a second canopy out of breath and Sousa
Up to the sun, out to the farthest row
As down the river that had seemed a street
Floated ships as many-tiered as wedding cakes
Barges freighted with Indians and trappers
4-H queens like prairie Cleopatras
Bearded fathers as calmly regal

As Abraham setting out from Ur,
Until at the very end the Ark itself—
Pigs, chickens, geese, sheep and stunned old Noah
Transformed by so many thousand children's eyes
Into the vessel of the world redeemed—
Sailed into her bedazzled heart
Towing in its wake who else
But cartwheeling you, you clowns?

You clowns with faces whiter than angels' clothes:
How did she know what made you fly?
Perhaps your flapping checkered pants,
Baggy shirts with buttons fat as jet-suit studs
Simplified your bodies, translated
Flesh to synonyms of wind.
Or like the peaked, starred hats of wizards
Did battered hoboes' caps yank you
Right off a world turned trampoline
To soar above her head, then tumble
In looping dives back down to earth
Which bounced you laughing back up to splash
And swim in honey-colored air?
Maybe something in your fingers
Flicked gravity clean away
And spun oranges, eggs and bowling pins
Between your legs, up to the sky and down
To nest like tamed falcons in pockets
Big enough to swallow any law?
Or for all she knew it was something else—
The way you rolled your diamonded eyes
To tickle from the crowd a unanimity of joy:
Did they conjure thickened air into people-webs?
Or did your improbable lips stretch
Words into invisible balloons hoisting you
Free from every downward pull?
Anyway she knew

You had her heart whirling with the oranges
Tossing her so lightly back and forth as you
flew
That her weightless body did triples and
Unbelievable quadruples at the very peak,
You clowns, of the flawless midsummer sky.

So flying that free, you clowns, how could
she doubt
When you spotted the round arena roof
Slick as a mountain of topaz and sapphire,
Pointed and beat your chests, that you could
Hurdle such an anthill in a single bound?
When you, clown, knelt flexing your muscles
And you, clown, pawed the earth and began
your sprint,
How could she laughing have held her
breath?
And oh clown! You had it timed so right,
Pushed with your foot just as you felt the lift
And leaped as casual as any angel
Holding your hat, amazed yourself
Daedelus in motley soaring up the roof's
curve
Half-way, higher, more, shouting –
Then began to fall, mouth still wide,
Slid, sprawled, thudded
On the suddenly solid ground.

Clown: a heap of rags, a pratfall –
Then once again a somersault
A flyer back-flipping down the street
Slapping the golden dust from your rear
Celebrating mortality.
They all got it – twirlers, trappers, pioneers
Cleopatras, Indians, Noah –
All the kids, but her.
Couldn't you have guessed, you clowns?
When gravity won, her soul lost;
Her spirit's banged coccyx made her
Scream rain right up into the cloudless sky.

So no matter how you capered and pranked
She hid her eyes, weeping, disenchanted
Unwilling to give you a second look;
You'd juggled her heart like a new egg
And let it fall, splat on the hard earth.
Clowns.

O Jesus, you clown:
You clattered down the cross
And fell with such a thud the world shook.
A twisted heap of flesh in Mary's lap
Your coil of words unsprung
Flat out of fancy leaps. . . .
You used to flick death away with a smile
Now Magdalen's tears puddle on your chest.
John paraded after you, begging for tricks—
Fire from heaven, multiplied fish, word-
  struck seas—
But now he knew nothing would hurt again
Unless he tried to laugh.

Only Mary got it.
However that was—Cana maybe
When glory and water became wine
To launch a party beyond the stars,
Probably even before when she felt
Your baby hands mold her heart into shapes
She'd never imagined, worlds without end—
She bent the pain like a rubber sword
And got it: whatever goes down must
  come up.
Right, Jesus? O clown!

Jesus! You mastered it with such grace.
Your flesh sleighter than the guards'
  befuddled eyes
Light from your newly naked face spilled
  out,
Gathered in pools on the once solid ground
Caught Magdalen's tears, cleansed her eyes
Your feet so still now she could see

They moved too fast for her hugging arms
Your hands made so deft by the holes
That birds, galaxies, mountains, hearts
Sailed into place just so, at last
Your lucid face in perpetual solstice –
No strings attached, no magic needed,
  human –
Your eyes holding all in motion, still
Pulling out of ten trillion souls and bodies
A unanimity of joy.

                        You clown, Jesus,
And what a sight to see you clowning still
Patting the dust into gold
Kissing hard earth into flesh, just so
Celebrating gravity and light agility at once
And by the patient fingers of your voice
Coaxing scared hands away from eyes
To see our splattered selves whole again
And whirling motionlessly as God,
Laughing with all the children of morning
To see ourselves bounce back with you
Clowning flawlessly all eternity away.

4 THINGS AS THEY ARE

ORDINARY TIME

In one of my earliest conscious memories I am standing in the back yard on a cloudless summer day. I am about four years old, and I am looking up into the shoreless blue of the sky. I ask: "Is that where God lives?"

I do not remember the answer, except that it was kind. I do not even remember why I asked the question, except that it seems a perfectly logical question. Faced with shorelessness, bathed in sunlight, wouldn't anyone, especially a child, think of God? What seems remarkable to me now is not that I asked that question when I was four, but that I have failed to ask it so often in the forty years since. What else is there to know?

Some people best see God's face in the immaculate stillness of winter, when a silent, universal white breathes with the hidden fullness of sound and color. Many others know him when the earth stirs and sends forth a million green messages in every square yard of grass, or when, with every tree a burning bush, autumn launches their souls across the brown fields of the dying year into the unchanging beauty of his splendor. As for me, when the sun stands highest, still, at the very peak of summer to fill the earth, the sky, my heart with an ocean of light so vast that it seems almost endless, it is then that I know even in my body that God has made his home here, with us, in this passing world. Summer, I will always think, is truly ordinary time.

Think of it: for these very days and weeks, so plain, so common that like the public schools in New York City they are numbered, not named, the extraordinary feasts and seasons have happened — just as it is for all the seemingly ordinary days since the first Pentecost that the Word became flesh, lived, preached, suffered, died, rose, ascended, and sent forth the Spirit. Because we do not see, and because we need parties and because we do not see what the parties are meant to enable us to see, we usually get it just backward. Nothing too much in the cosmic order is going on today, we think; it is only the Eighteenth Sunday in Ordinary Time; or five days before the Assumption; or such a long time until Christmas; green vestments still. Yes, green vestments still and forever, *per omnia saecula saeculorum!* The purple and the white, the rose and the red are for the *sake* of the green. God made Bethlehem and Nazareth happen, willed the cross, the tomb, Easter, the glorification of his Son at his right hand for the sake of ordinary time, that it might one day bloom into truly endless summer, its green becoming in the alchemy of the apocalypse pure, living gold.

Let me put it another way, in the words of Lewis Thomas's marvelous book, *The Lives of a Cell:*

> Statistically, the probability of any one of us being here is so small that you'd think the mere fact of existing would keep us all in a contented dazzlement of surprise. We are alive against the stupendous odds of genetics.... The normal, predictable state of matter throughout the universe is randomness.... We, in brilliant contrast, are completely organized structures....catching electrons at the moment of their excitement by solar photons, swiping the energy released at the instant of each jump and storing it up in intricate loops for ourselves.... Add to this the biological improbability that makes each member of our own species unique. ... One in [five] billion...a self-contained, free-standing individual, labeled by specific protein configurations at the surfaces of cells, identifiable by whorls of fingertip skin, maybe even by special medleys of fragrance. You'd think we'd never stop dancing.[1]

Stop? Most of us never start. Dr. Thomas gently suggests that we are overly familiar with our amazingly improbable being and only just beginning to develop the experience of world-wide communion necessary for lasting celebration. He has a point. With Teilhard de Chardin and others, I sense that recognizing and harnessing the energies of love could mean a second discovery of fire—the fire the Master came to cast upon the earth and spoke of when he promised that our joy would be full. But I am not surprised that most people are not yet surprised into joy by life. I do not wonder that most of those who believe in God do not dance in wonderment. I am not even puzzled that most Christians are not bedazzled by the glory of the ordinary. Do they burst into song and delighted laughter at the consecration? Then why expect them to clap their hands and shout

[1]Lewis Thomas, *The Lives of a Cell.* pp. 165-166.

for joy on a hot, sticky, gasless summer morning?

No, there are 50 or 150 good reasons why most people, even most Christians, don't really get it, except now and again, and once boiled down, all those reasons become one: they haven't heard the Good News. But what about us who have? What about us whose eyes the Holy Spirit has enlightened, whose hearts he has broken open – who know Jesus as living Master and intimate companion, who experience, imperfectly but truly, God as merciful Abba, who have been washed and healed and forgiven, who have tasted the bread of life and drunk from the cup of gladness, not blindly but with startling clarity? What about us whose tears have been dried by the Mother of God, who have chatted with the saints, feasted on Scripture, watched as our very own crippled psyches began to heal again? We who have been plunged by God's own design into Easter, who have felt the Good News ricocheting down our bloodstream, who have even found Alleluias on our lips on gray Monday mornings: do we shine with what we see within us, all around us?

As an image of joy, dancing has its limitations. We will be doing very well if we dance when the Lord tells us to – at times of extraordinary joy or extraordinary persecution. But we have not finished with the question of celebrating ordinary time once we've decided that shouts of gladness at the office or dances of praise around the kitchen are not usually what St. Paul had in mind when he told us to rejoice in the Lord always (Phil 4:4). I used to think that the reason even we Christians who have truly heard the Gospel have such difficulty in showing forth the joy of the risen Lord day after ordinary day was deeply mysterious. After all, I simply had to look at myself: such a clear command and such a shabby performance. It is easy enough to understand why we don't rejoice when the time is made extraordinary by sudden death, grave illness, an abrupt meeting with a new depth of grief or injustice; it's just too hard. But what of all the other moments? It is true that we need inner healing, even after Jesus becomes real for us, to be able to experience his loving presence in places of our being long darkened by the hurts of the past. Even more, we need spiritual healing, especially from a false notion of the cross, which confuses gloominess with compassion and which twists our gaze away from the free gift of life given by the crucified and risen Lord and focuses instead on our own pain as the coin of salvation. My father was not a religious man, but he knew enough to laugh at my somber foolishness when, at the age of five or six, I asked why "Good" Friday wasn't called "Bad." Most of us need to learn that lesson over and over until, with St. Paul, we are so immersed in the power of Christ's resurrection that we *joyfully* ask for a share in his sufferings (Phil 3:10).

Yet while it still seems obvious to me that we fear abandonment and embarrassment, that we need many sorts of healing, I begin to suspect that the reason most Christians do not find ordinary green synonymous with joy is not so very mysterious. I begin to think that we simply have not looked with real care at ordinary sunlight, or if we have, have not tried very hard to walk in the light we have seen. I hear the Master saying to me, "Unless you turn and become like a child, you cannot enter the kingdom of heaven" (Mt 18:3).

I've been pondering this word in my heart for a good many years now, and I can't know one-billionth of what it means, but surely Jesus is telling us to be where we are—here, in this place, on this day, at this moment, now. A child doesn't know any other way to be, but learning to live that way again takes patience, practice, and as Catherine's prayer says, awesome courage[2]—to let go, to let time happen, to "kiss the joy as it flies," as William Blake put it. True, the more vividly one knows the Lord who lives within, the easier it is to seek him without; but if one looks and listens and smells and touches, is it possible not to meet him whose blood has made every leaf, every bird, every human face new? If I let my face be what it is, a child's face, how can I not meet him whose face is like mine?

The earth, as Emily cries out in *Our Town*,[3] is indeed too wonderful for anyone to realize; never mind the earth—the dullest day, the plainest human face. But one Christian did realize, grasp, celebrate, live every moment of life, and it is deeply right that we keep the feast of her home-going in mid-August, at the heart of summer, in the depths of ordinary time. Her whole being went home to the fullness of the Kingdom where she had always lived; but because Mary kept every word God gave her, in her heart and in her life, the earth forever holds her fragrance.[4] She has become a sachet of her Son's love, hidden not only along streams and in green meadows, but in every corner of every ordinary house, along every hot sidewalk, in the bowels of every slum. The poor know it. Ask them.

---

[2]"Give me the heart of a child, and the awesome courage to live it out."

[3]Thornton Wilder, *Our Town*, Acting Edition. (New York: Coward-McCann, Inc., 1938), p. 83.

[4]Rainer Maria Rilke, "Of the Death of Mary," Translations from the poetry of Rainer Maria Rilke, by M. D. Herter Norton (New York: W. W. Norton & Company, 1962), part 3.

Better still, ask her yourself where her Son lives—in the shoreless sky, in the fathomless heart, in the impenetrable day, in the unbearable pain. Ask her now, ask her at the hour of your death, ask her every moment in between. Say: "Here, Mother Mary? Here? Is he here too?" And she will say, "Yes, of course, yes"—and smile gently with you like the morning star heralding the new day.

THE TRANSFIGURING CROSS

In the inexhaustible joy of his love the Father wills to transfigure the whole universe with the glory shining now in Jesus, his Son. The glory that was his before the foundation of the world now radiates through every cell of his risen body and, more calmly than the morning sun fills all our air with light, his Spirit bears that glory into the hidden core of every sub-atomic particle and across all the light-years to the remotest galaxy at creation's expanding edge. Most deeply of all, the life-creating Spirit transfigures us, and every other race in the cosmos like us, into flawless icons of our glorious Christ. "See what love the Father has given us, that we should be called the children of God; and so we are.... Beloved, we are God's children now; it does not yet appear what we shall be, but we know that when he appears we shall be like him, for we shall see him as he is" (1 Jn 3:1-2).

Our imaginations fall apart when we try to picture all creation radiant with the light now shining on the face of Christ. How can we say what it will look like when every human face burns with the unburning fire of the Holy Trinity? When every relationship, every civilization, people of every race and tongue and planet glow with uncreated splendor? When the Church at long last is revealed as the immaculate bride of Jesus? When we are wholly one in the never-ending happiness of God, and all sadness has forever vanished? To imagine that—no more division, no more war, no more disease, no more misunderstanding, no more waste, no more good-byes, no more loneliness, no more poverty, no more sin, no more pain, and no more, never again, death—is quite beyond our power.

But not beyond the Father's. "Blessed are the pure of heart, for they shall see God." (Mt 5:1). He gives us hearts of true flesh, reborn flesh, and eyes such as his eyes would be if he had bodily eyes, eyes such as he gave Peter, James, and John on Mt. Tabor, eyes like the eyes of his

Son, Jesus: eyes as clear as glory. Even before our healing is finished, as medicine, in fact, for our hearts' healing, he gives us images of what we shall soon fully be: the Master transfigured on Mt. Tabor, Mary lifted bodily, as securely and as tenderly as once she lifted her Son, into his glory.

It will be, then, as we look at the Lord and his Mother, a little bit like this: to be clothed like the New Jerusalem in a morning brightness that never fades; to know no darkness in heart or mind or emotions; to feel no darkness in any gesture of love; to taste no darkness in memory or intelligence; to hear no darkness in the will; to be clothed in light that gathers the sun of every season we have known into the seasonless glory of the Trinity. It will be something like this:

To receive from the Master the gift of his own freedom. To stand forth at last as a truly human person, without shackles, free of all the lies that told us we were locked in competition with God. Free of fear, free of guilt and self-hatred, free of the ache of egotism, free to see the serenity of God's freedom. Then, no longer groping blindly for God, longing for him but always missing him because we had never known how to reach without grasping, the promises of hope will be poured out into our laps—full measure, pressed down, overflowing.

To love. To see—not just for a moment, but always—the beauty of our brothers, our sisters. No longer called to wipe away their tears or to wash their feet, but at last free simply to enjoy them, to be with them, never again to be separated. To understand and to be understood; to be delivered forever of the gloom of loneliness and self-pity; to have the desert of our solitude bloom with the presence of God and all his children.

To know the Mother of God and all the saints as God knows them. Not touching for only brief flashes the beauty of Mary, of the holy ones, of the angels, but to know them in their full magnificence, but intimately, and to know from their love and delight that we too have become as glorious as they. And to know what it is to rejoice in one's own beauty and the beauty of others without envy or shame because all that joy flows forth from and back into God's own incorruptible, Triune delight.

And above all, to receive from Jesus the gift of worship, the fullness of adoration, where "I" and "we" are no longer divided. To fall down before the Father as our hearts hunger to, but have not known how, to be swept away by his holiness and to find our true life before him, his child, his beloved. To see Jesus face to face. To feel his eyes eternally on our faces, to have the joy of knowing that nothing will separate us, forever. To be lost in wonder at his glory and to be perfectly at home in his heart. To discover there, at the very center of God, the unveiled face of the Holy Spirit.

For as many years as I've been a Catholic, and perhaps even before that, I have known that this transfiguration has already begun. Any confirmation of that knowledge from the wisdom of the Church—not only in its saints, its liturgies, its theologies, but in its little ones, those who bring their food to church to be blessed on Holy Saturday, or those who used to go by the tens of thousands to bathe in the ocean on the Feast of the Assumption—has given me joy, but that joy has only echoed what the Lord himself showed me on the night of my first Communion.

It has always seemed clear, and saints both far away and very close at hand have convinced me that it is so, that if we could let the Lord teach us to look at his cross with his own eyes, nothing any longer could resist the tide of transfiguration in us. We have learned, at least a little, to see the glory of the risen Lord in beauty, and that vision gives us joy. But perfect joy, complete transformation, lies in knowing that in Jesus the Father has transfigured pain and death and sin itself.

There is a mystery here so simple that only the risen eyes of the Master can reveal its meaning. Pain begins in a refusal of love. Every pain suffered by every human began with someone's refusal to love or to accept love. The Father meant us to live in a world filled with his love, a world in which men and women would experience no pain, no sorrow, no loss, no death: none. In a way we cannot grasp fully, our ancient parents said no to God's love, and in saying no to the fullness of love, pain came. That is also how pain has entered into our own lives. Others have said no, refused to love us, and we have refused to love them, and we have received our inheritance of pain and death.

Yet it is as if the Lord Jesus says this about his cross: "I have touched your pain. I have entered every refusal of love, and each act of non-love I have embraced. I have pressed it into my body. I have become all pain. I have become all anguish. I have become all estrangement. I have become a curse. I have become ugliness. I have even become, in a way you will never understand, sin itself. I have taken it into me—into my flesh, into my heart, into my spirit, and as I took it into me, I made it something new. I took it into me because I love you, because the Father loves me, because he loves you. And until the end of time my cross stands before you as the great sign of what I have done to pain. It stands before you as the sign of my love forever, so that when you make the sign of the cross over yourself, you are baptized in my love, you are plunged into my life, you are immersed with me in the Father."

And he says this, too, it seems: "My cross is a sign of my Father's love for you. You cannot hear the tears of God because they are too mysterious for the ears and the minds of human beings, but my passion is my Father's passionate love for you. I am the infinite joy of my Father, but he was *glad* to see me die because he loves you so much, because your suffering is such an abomination to him that he could not bear you to endure it. In my heart he embraced all refusal to love, and filled it with my yes to him and to you, so that what was death has become life and what was nothing has become a work of love."

Finally, it seems as if the Master says this with an infinitely deep voice: "I share with you the secret of my heart and the secret of my Father's heart, so that you can share the fullness of our love. If I could have had you with me when I spoke the stars and the moons and the planets and everything on them into being, I would have had you with me. I could not, but now, when I am speaking a new creation into being in the heart of every person on this earth and throughout the universe, now when my love is redeeming all sin and transfiguring all pain, now I call you to be with me, to embrace what I embrace, to share with me the joy of loving as I love. Don't be afraid! I want you to know the joy of bringing life out of death. I want you to know the joy of seeing light come forth from darkness. I want you to be the bearers of my resurrection in your own flesh. I want you to know the joy of God whose work is to make men and women live. I want you to know that the ugliness that has attached itself to you so closely that you cannot ever rid yourself of it is no longer what it seems to be. I have so embraced your refusal to love and so soaked you with light that you are becoming all light. So, my brothers, my sisters, take up my cross, the cross of the poor, and let me make you one with me as you become one with them. I will make you one with my Father, and in my Spirit you will know and love us as we know and love you. And God's joy will be your joy."

As the living knowledge of the Lord's transfiguring cross cleanses my heart and gives me new eyes, I think of Agnes Sanford's prayer: "Lord Jesus Christ, receive me into Thy own glorified being that I may abide with Thee." "Words," she says, "are not great enough to describe that sense of walking about in a body of light that is not our own, but is his light."[1] Words are not great enough to proclaim the Good News that Jesus lives, that he lives in us so that even now we are transfigured children of God.

No words can encompass this mystery of joy, but once, over twenty-five years ago, my heart burst into song as I saw, a little, how the dark moment of Calvary had transformed the whole universe into Tabor:

Beauty is hiding in secret places
In earth-marred hands and fetid bins
In joy surprised in down-turned faces
In souls disclosed by griefs and sins.

Beauty is burning in sorrow's coldness
Is blooming in soil of stony night.
Beauty is bursting from death and oldness
In flowers of splendor and light.

O earth reborn! O heart made new!
What midnights saw you rise?
O secret Tabor blossoming fast,
O morning white with dew!
Did you—Lazarus, brother, in dead man's guise—
Dance at feel, beneath your feet, of grass?

Night is far advanced. The morning's star shines like a great diamond at the throat of the dawn. The love of Christ has washed the whole world clean. Day is at hand.

---

[1]Agnes Sanford, *Behold Your God* (St. Paul, MN: Macalester Park Publishing Company, 1958), p.125.

describe that sense of walking about in a body of light that is not our own, but in his hand.[illegible] Words are not great enough to proclaim the [illegible] that leaps [illegible] us so that [illegible] we [illegible] distinguish [illegible] different [illegible].

No words can encompass this mystery of Divinity, once, over twenty-five years ago, and [illegible] as I saw a little, how [illegible] the whole universe into [illegible]:

Beauty is hiding in secret places
[illegible]
[illegible] face
[illegible]
Beauty is [illegible] in [illegible] loneliness
[illegible]
Beauty [illegible] from [illegible] darkness
In flowers of [illegible] and lights.
O [illegible] Thou [illegible] now!
[illegible]
O [illegible]
O morning [illegible]
[illegible]
[illegible]

[illegible] like a great diamond [illegible] the whole world [illegible] hand.

[illegible] (New York: [illegible] Publishing Company [illegible]).

WITH THE NAKED EYE

On a clear night in the late summer or early fall you can see in the eastern sky the Andromeda Nebula, really a spiral galaxy like our own and the only one that can be spotted with the naked eye. It is twice as large as our own—contains, that is, twice as many billions of stars as the Milky Way. It appears as a small faint smudge a little above the second star from Pegasus, in the constellation Andromeda, which lies in early fall just below the giant "W" of Casseopeia. This galaxy is the most distant object the unaided human eye can see. It floats in the dark ocean of space more than two million light-years away.

Two million light-years. The silence of the nearly immeasurable interstellar spaces revealed by the revolutionary vision of Galileo frightened Pascal. That silence fills me with adoration. As I look toward Andromeda, my naked eyes see a light that is older than the human race in its present form. My eyes grow older than all our history. Yet as they peer back beyond human time to see a light that began to shine before our first parents sinned, they grow young. In that faint, quiet smudge they see an icon of the serene and fathomless purity of God.

Catherine has often written of our nostalgia for Eden. It is a longing not for the simplicities of childhood, but for the purity that would have enabled us to see, in our own way, as clearly as God sees. Still, when October comes, and I am another year older; when I look with eyes as naked as possible at all the birthdays I can remember, I understand how the innocence, however fragmented, that we once knew can be a symbol for that other, deeper innocence. For all of us there was a time, brief perhaps, flawed certainly, when we were naked and neither afraid nor ashamed. But to see that time we do need naked eyes: eyes lighted not by stars only, but by faith.

Often it is simpler to see the unspoiled light of a life other than one's own. As I pray with people, I can "see" it in them: the radiance of lives taking shape in the womb, each of them, no matter who the parents, a visible image of the Father's sovereign and all-creating Word. Baptism, of course, fills the child with a brilliance greater than any supernova, but even before, light is already shining because the Word made flesh has breathed forth the Spirit of life into all creation. When you see that life, with the eyes of faith, you know that God sees it and proclaims it very good – not immaculate like Mary's, but very good, able to be made fully pure by the same love that fashioned her into a new Eden for a new Adam.

Mary: when I think of my eyes becoming naked, I think of her. Once, many years ago at Mass, her gaze cut through the swirl of the ritual and the busy traffic of my own soul, and I stood in stillness, more naked than a child: as naked as Adam. In the Christian East they say that you can see the Holy Spirit's face in her eyes. Yes; and in the face and heart of Jesus toward whom she is always looking, whether in the glory of the Father or in the center of our hearts.

Another time, more recently, a priest told me that he asked the Father to show him the deepest truth of his – the priest's – being. As he descended down into his inner self, he was ready for a word of either reproach or blessing. He only wanted to know the truth. But the word God spoke was vaster than any blessing and more revealing than any reproach. When he reached the very center of his life, my friend heard God say, "Jesus."

Somehow – by the indescribable grace of her motherhood – Mary never let me out of her sight. Even when my eyes were too weak to keep my self in focus or too sick to see at all, she saw me, and Jesus used her seeing to heal me and to give me naked eyes again, faith-eyes, child's eyes. I feared I would never hear the Father speak my true name, never see the face of my Lord while I lived, but in the purity of Mary's sight I have come to see. In the stillness of her love I have come to hear.

October is coming, and I think of the way I used to wake up smiling on my birthday – as if on the bright side of the night some lovely secret awaited to surprise me. I see now that the secret I felt the day would show me was more than attention, more than joy, more even than the love I would have gladly settled for. I was waiting for a sacred day and the revelation of the children of God. I see too that the revelation was always given me, though I scarcely knew it, for my birthdays shine in my memory like a string of beads as shiny and as many-colored as October itself. Each of them is a psalm of praise "for the wonder of my being," and as they pass through my heart, I see that the revelation I longed for was given as I fingered not only my birthdays, but the beads of all my days until all of them, the ordinary as well as the joyful, the saddest as well as the most glorious, became mere events no longer, but mysteries.

A rosary of praise. Did I think, all those years ago when I first began to say the rosary, that I was learning to see my own life, as well as the life of my Master and Lord, with naked eyes? Perhaps I did, a little. I remember how the mysteries wove themselves into my brain, into my flesh, until I no longer thought about them, but breathed their atmosphere as naturally as I breathed the earth's air. Whatever I realized then, I know now that the Spirit of God, through the prayers of Mary, was breathing in me to teach me the Gospel names for all the days of my life.

The real Galilean revolution took place in the first century, not in the sixteenth. A man came walking out of Galilee, and his eyes were so clear that if anyone let his look in, it healed the heart and showed forth the glory of the Kingdom shining, within and without, even more simply than the everyday sun. So much clarity, too much for some, and they tried to stuff his light into the black hole of death. But might as well pour the Milky Way into a bag: on the third day the Master came forth from darkness as calmly as he had from Galilee, changing darkness itself into the brightness of day without end. Now his eyes could reach to the end of time and space to lift the veil from every heart and to give to all creatures the glorious revelation of the children of God.

I look toward him, toward Jesus, my Master, and I behold his glory, and I see all my days pass into his eyes so that I too may "be changed into his likeness from glory to glory" (2 Cor 3:18). My eyes are not naked yet, my heart not wholly unveiled, but if I am willing, each day becomes my bright October birthday, the image of Christ's unutterably beautiful face. His compassion makes me what he is, and his joy teaches me to sing, without embarrassment or shyness, the song my whole being will sing the day that my body rises with the whole reborn creation. And if I am willing to let the light of his face keep shining into me, no matter what the cost, to let his Spirit speak his name in me with every breath, my eyes will become his eyes, and wherever I look, I will look into the face of God.

DISTINGUISHING MARKS

When you apply for a job or a passport, the forms ask, along with questions concerning age, rank, and social security number, "Distinguishing marks?" The first time I had to answer, I wondered if they were interested in the small moles on my neck and collarbone. Did they want to know about the scar under my lower lip, where I had cut myself at five when I was showing off by pulling a load of kids in a cart my grandfather had made for us, and tripped and skidded a bit, face down, on the pavement? I decided not, and when I consulted experts (e.g., my mother), I was told, no, of course not, they were thinking of birthmarks, deformities, wounds, or – God forbid – tattoos.

I wasn't wholly persuaded. The forms seemed a bit like those irritating multiple choice tests where the answer most nearly fitting the definition is only marginally more plausible than a second, possibly more creative, response. Still, it did seem likely that neither the government nor an employer wanted a detailed tour of the surfaces of my body, and I have continued, even as life has marked my flesh more and more assertively, to deny that the process had distinguished me in any way.

But surely it has. Surely that is what life is always up to – not just separating sheep from goats, but marking each sheep and each goat until each is recognizable fully as itself and no other. Surely my markings are by this time as unmistakable to an observer of humanflesh as are horses' shades of color, whorls of hair, configurations of bone, and daubs of white to experts in horseflesh. Who else has life imprinted precisely as it has me – left shin neatly scarred by ski-accident, crook of left arm faintly pocked by boil now more than 40 years gone, shoulder and neck and chest creased just so by scalpels, barely decipherable scar over eyebrow, souvenir of a humiliating fall on an icy New Haven sidewalk? Not to speak of gray hairs caused by certain well-defined meetings of stress, genes, and choice; of dimples turning into creases; of skin around eyes pouching and wrinkling. "Age and age's evils, hoar hair, / Ruck and wrinkle, drooping, dying," as Hopkins' "Leadon Echo" goes; or as my aunt used to say, "Sags and bags, sags and bags."

On the surface, of course, my marking has only begun, but when the first leaves begin to fall, you don't need to be a prophet to foresee the naked trees. Besides, on all of us the rucks and sags of the surface only hint at the invisible wrinkling that began in us on the day of our birth when our skin was, and would be for years, as smooth as new butter or May skies. While our faces remained vague and undefined, fear and sorrow molded the features of our hearts, loss shaped our spirits, and our first knowledge of love fashioned in us a secret image of joy. If I touch my cheek, I feel nothing like those marks on the face of the Cure d'Ars as deep as wounds, but where I cannot reach with my fingers, into my soul, I know that life has carved my being in ways so intricate that not even angels' eyes can read their pattern. But as life carves away on us, it carves away life as it shapes both flesh and spirit. We are reduced to uniqueness as a preparation for death.

Rilke's poem "Autumn": "The leaves are falling, falling, as from way off, / As though far gardens withered in the sky."[1] We too are endlessly falling "past all the stars" in our utter uniqueness, like leaves in an interminable autumn, like the soundless flakes of snow falling everywhere in James Joyce's story, "The Dead," covering with singularly marked fragments of flesh, of spirit, the earth that falls endlessly too. Is anyone there to catch us? Are there hands that hold our falling, eyes that mark the passage of each bit of marked being, each sparrow-like atom?

We say yes, God holds us, the God whose ineffable right hand has become flesh in Jesus. Yes, we say: the God who made us knowing we would fall, who willed that we be made of such stuff that might fall away and then fall endlessly down, is a Father who holds our falling in a love like hands that never weary. We say more: that this love, which willed even before we fell to mark our inmost faces with the weight and the beauty of the earth and its passing, now wills to lift us by the beautiful weight of the Easter flesh of Jesus Christ into the light that knows no setting.

And more than this: look — not with eyes or imagination, but with

---

[1]Rilke, p. 75.

faith—at the Master. With faith, you'd know him anywhere, no matter how the evil one might seek to confuse you. "I know mine, and mine know me" (John 10:14), says the Master, the good shepherd. But what do you know? The glory of his Godhead? The splendor of his eternal Sonship? His eyes like a flaming fire? With faith, yes, of course, but the light of the Father shining in Jesus and in us to reveal him as true God from true God, everlasting Lord, almighty Word with almighty Father, shines not just on or through, but in the face of Jesus. The immortal and omnipotent Word of God has a human face forever. The Master will never be done with his body.

What do you know, then, when you look at Jesus in faith? You know the full glory of God shining in human flesh. You know how the thorn-scratches, healed now into faint flecks of white against the living skin, gleam like a second halo across his forehead. You know where sun as well as resurrection has polished his hair and his throat, where earth and wood have shaped his fingers and callused his palms. You look at his hands (or maybe his wrists), back and front, and you know that in those shallow scars a whole universe's pain disappeared. If you touched his side, you would feel the pulse of God pumping through human blood from a human heart that learned to beat in a woman's womb, was imprinted at birth with the shape of her face, was marked by tears, his own and others', and one April afternoon fell slowly, very agonizingly still.

Jesus has his Mother's eyes. Everyone who has ever looked into them with faith says so. But maybe you can notice how the summer sun of Galilee, reflecting from the wheatfields and the lake, has crinkled them at the edges. You see how free they are, serene, and you must realize how that freedom comes not only from the sight of glory, but, along with the fine bones of his face, from his Mother and all his ancestors. Love made his eyes' peace, grace that worked through generations of human time as well as in an instant of eternity. But as you look into that clear gaze, you see that it has encompassed everything. Through those eyes all the tears of the world have fallen into the joy of God, and, transfigured there, they come streaming back, the early morning light of an everlasting spring. Time itself is born again.

Everything about the Master is like this, radiantly cruciform. You see it, don't you? You can hear it in his voice, planed just so by his cries to his people, shaped precisely by his people's cries to him since time began—Babylon, Masada, Auschwitz; Hiroshima, the Boyne, Gettysburg, Thermopylae. If you can catch his scent—bright fall leaves and newly plowed fields, a hint of salt and the fragrance of breakfast cooking on a beach—you can even smell it: goodness ripened like grapes in Burgundy, crushed and ground in the winepress, fermented some place cool and out of the sun, uncorked at table and filling the room with summer and with laughter. Most of all you can hear it in the sound of his voice, human and eternal Word made one, eternally spoken in the Father's silence, moving through the intricately wrought spaces of his human soul, dying into stillness on the cross, then rising on Easter and forever like the roar of many waters, like the urgent call of bridegroom to his bride, "Come, beloved. Come to me and rest."

So it is that we glory "in the cross of our Lord Jesus Christ, through whom the world has been crucified to us and we to the world" (Gal 6:14). In him our falling is caught, held, ended. We bear on our bodies, psyches, hearts, and souls the marks of our Master, Jesus. We hear his voice, and we know him, and in that knowledge see the marks that distinguish us for what they truly are: the marks of his healing, life-giving, gloriously transforming cross. He has mastered time. Our losses become wombs of light. Torn and aging flesh becomes the seed of a body that will outshine the sun. Marks of carelessness and ignorance and especially sin, washed and cleansed in the blood of the Lamb, gleam like the radiant mouths of angels with songs of praise to the tenderness of God. The fragments that apparently Christless life has carved away are sealed, each one, with the sign of Christ's victory, and as they pass through his hands, they are fashioned by the Spirit into the all-holy Body that is the fullness of the glory of Jesus the Lord.

And on that hidden place in us, where love first formed the secret image of our joy, God smiles in the face of his Son, and the dust stirs, as it stirred on the first human morning—all the siftings of our disappointments, all the fragments of our forgetfulness, all the atoms of our longing, all marked and each distinguished by the sign of Love—and Love makes us, now or very soon, what he is: joy without end.

LOVING AND LETTING GO

"We are strangers before you, and sojourners, as were all our fathers. Our days on the earth are as a shadow, and there is no abiding" (1 Chr 29:15). So David the King prayed as he let his life go back to God. But listen to St. Paul, whose own eyes had seen the King who died and rose and lives forever in the Father's glory:

> We do not lose heart. Though outwardly we are wasting away, yet inwardly we are being renewed day by day. For our light and momentary troubles are achieving for us an eternal glory that far outweighs them all. So we fix our eyes not on what is seen, but on what is unseen. For what is seen is passing away, but what is unseen lasts forever (2 Cor 4:16-18).

You feel it most sharply in the fall—"Margaret, are grieving at Goldengrove's unleaving?"—when leaves let go, when light and warmth fade, when distances widen everywhere. You don't even have to known anything about entropy and the second law of thermodynamics to understand that all flesh is grass, that the sun itself is burning up, that life never stops telling us to let go. When the mild light of October has passed across your skin enough times, you know that "life could never be long enough to hold all the summer evenings [you] would like to enjoy."[1]

But even if we were not outwardly wasting away, even if the sun stood still for an endless succession of moments, so that summer never ended and life never dwindled, it would still be true that only what is unseen lasts forever. The secularized mind dreams of conquering physical death and toys with sanitized forms of reincarnation (e.g., no coming back as a beetle or a leper). Yet those who have been caught in the snares of that myth for 3500 years or more know that reincarnation is only another way, one of the worst, of being

[1]Richard Adams, *Nature through the Seasons* (London: Penguin, 1976), p. 12.

locked away from that unseen life that cannot pass away. As Leon Bloy insisted, we are all pilgrims of the Absolute. All of us, like St. Augustine, yearn for the Beauty, timeless and always new, that is our only lasting home.

How do we get there? The Master told us clearly. He is the one Way to the eternal beauty that is the Father. He empowers us to move to the Father by so uniting himself with us in the Spirit that, if we want, we can live *his* life, see with *his* eyes, love with *his* heart. And what does this mean? He tells us: "Love one another as I have loved you" (Jn 15:12).

This way of resurrection is so simple; this way of the cross is so agonizing. The more we try to love another, to share this person's life, to embrace that person's flesh in marriage, to experience this one in another way in friendship and humble service in order to know the unchanging presence of God in all this amazing and changing flesh – the more love we live, the more certainly we must let it all be carried away on the cross and brought back from the tomb by Christ himself, whose power and goodness we can scarcely find words for, much less manipulate or control. We Christians are certainly not Platonists, but the essence of the human person – never mind God! – is so mysterious that to open ourselves to that inner core of another's being seems to leave behind everything we love most in her or him. All that we love most – bright hair, face in repose, pitch of the voice speaking our name, eyes where childhood still lives, features shining with unique light, body shaped just this way and no other – is passing away. We cannot hold that beauty unless we let it go; yet what love is this that asks love's end?

We are not Platonists, but Plotinus, one of the greatest Platonists of them all, understood that to see one must let go of earthly light and walk in what seems at first darkness to the mind. He told his disciples: "There are parts of what it most concerns you to know that I cannot describe to you. You must come with me and see for yourselves." Long before, Christ our Master spoke of that place of stillness on the other side of death and made himself the way to it by our own passage into and back from darkness:

> Where I am going, you cannot follow now, but you will follow later.... Do not let your hearts be troubled. Trust in God; trust also in me. There are many rooms in my Father's house; ... I am going there to prepare a place for you. And if I go and prepare a place for you, I will come back and take you to be with me that you also may be where I am" (Jn 13:36, 14:1-3).

All my life I have struggled to travel this passage into the unseen. Why do we Christians call it "detachment"? It is simply death and resurrection. What "it most concerns us to know" is how to lay hold of the Kingdom Christ has won for us; or to use the words he spoke in the "Little Mandate" of Madonna House, how to love without counting the cost, how to go into the depths of human hearts without fear so that we can be with him, not just at the end of time, but now. It is Jesus the Master who is the "how" of love — the way of love, the truth of love, the life of love. He is Love made flesh, and when he comes to us in the Spirit to love us into life without end, he molds our hearts into images of his own glorious and radiant cross.

One cold day, as the Lord prepared to take me with him to that place I could not reach without him, I was struggling once again with the mystery of love and the pain of love. I was feeling more than the darkness of celibate aloneness, of being faithful to my call not to make love and share my life in the ordinary way of marriage. I was living the anguish of knowing that the flesh and all its beauty is passing away into separation, decay, old age, death, and, worst of all, forgetfulness. That anguish cut with a special sharpness because I was experiencing it at the liturgy, where I was celebrating with all my brothers and sisters, seen and unseen, the victorious presence of Christ the Lord, who was drawing all of us into his own communion with the Father. I was celebrating oneness and experiencing aloneness.

Then, after I had received the Eucharist and was sitting outwardly in the bright Madonna House chapel but inwardly in the dim room of my narrow awareness, suddenly — I mean with the gentle opening of one's eyes after a long sleep — I "saw." The Lord within me touched my inner eyes, and I saw that all the beauty I had ever seen, especially in those I had loved, was simply the outer brightness of a deeper reality, not what we normally think of as the "soul" — something misty and insubstantial — but the spiritual *substance* that is the true core of the human person. I realized that all my life I had clutched at people because I couldn't bear to let go of the beauty of the seen — this moment, this flesh, that look or way of being. I realized that my "love" had often caused death because I would not let go. And suddenly I knew that if I *did* let go, not just once, but over and over and over again, I would always be traveling into the very center of the other, whomever I wanted to love, not leaving the body behind, but finding the source of its beauty in the unseen depths of the mystery we call "person." I was seeing the light of resurrection shining on

Christ's Body and on each of his members.

I saw that Jesus my Master was asking me to let go of regret and desire so that I could follow him to that deeper place, to embrace by not embracing the truly substantial reality, the beginning of an already risen self. As I let go and let my eyes, my heart, my being pass beyond all I could see and touch and hold, the sorrow of all my goodbyes would vanish too; and in the place I had always thought of as emptiness I would never have to say goodbye again. As the unseen Lord made his real presence known to my true eyes, as he taught me to stand still and alone in my own inmost being – where I already abide in him, "where everything in me is silent, and I am immersed in the silence of God"[2] – he would reveal to me the beauty in each person that is beyond withering and fading, where moth and rust cannot corrupt, where thief and time cannot break in and steal. I saw that my risen Master was offering his Kingdom, now: a communion in his Father's love where I would always be at home with all those I loved. Goodbyes would pass away because we would always be meeting – person to person, face to face – in God, in the unbounded exchange of love that is the Holy Trinity.

That day I "saw" these things not with the clarity of words, but of silence, where the dance of the still point shines so brightly that one forgets that learning its simple grace comes only in time. Yet I did see clearly and grasp for a moment the peace the Master promises those who trust him, the "peace that surpasses all understanding" (Phil 4:7). Later, words began to come to me as I remembered what St. Paul had written about the unseen life that does not pass away. I recalled Gerard Manley Hopkins's poems, "The Leaden Echo" and "The Golden Echo." Later still, in my new poustinia hidden under the pines on Madonna House's "island," I understood that it would take more tears than I had dreamed of to cleanse my eyes and make them true, to dissolve my death and uncover the life beneath it. Then, very much later, I came to know that I couldn't even "die," let go, unless the Master himself did it in me. It was then I saw that he had done more than "go away to prepare a place" for me; he had also come back to take me with him. "Eyeless, faceless, wordless" I might go – but only if I let Christ's unseen silence possess me.

> The world will not see me any more, but you will see me. Because I live, you also will live. On that day you will realize that I am in my Father, and you are in me, and I am in you. Whoever hears my

---

[2]Doherty, *Poustinia*, p.212.

> commands and obeys them, he is the one who loves me. He who loves me will be loved by my Father, and I too will love him and show myself to him. . . . My father will love him, and we will come to him and make our home with him" (Jn 14:19-21, 23).

Now, no matter how quickly earthly light fades or how vastly distances stretch, God is at home with us. The Father holds all our falling, and we fall always into his light—the light that this present world can neither see nor overcome. All is well: the Spirit does not leave us orphans. He gives us eyes to see the Father's glory shining on the face of Jesus and everywhere we look—in all things, in every heart, in our own. All is well: we begin to love with the love that cannot pass away.

THINGS AS THEY ARE

Another year is ending. Again the world is spinning toward the pole of darkness. Again I am looking through the center of that darkness to the place where the Church sees Jesus the Lord plunge into all the rivers of time and space to make by his presence each of our moments into a pool of baptism, a way into the Kingdom. From my vantage-point in ordinary time, where time is changed but not yet taken away, I am letting an old sun show me the eternal Day that the Church always celebrates, especially at Easter and at Christmas-Epiphany.

> Today the grace of the Holy Spirit ... comes down upon the waters. Today there shines the Sun that never sets, and the world is sparkling with the light of the Lord. Today the moon is bright, together with the earth, in its glowing radiance. Today the brilliant stars adorn the universe with splendor.... Today through the presence of the Lord the waters of the Jordan are changed into remedies. Today the whole universe is refreshed with mystical streams.... Today paradise has been opened to mankind, and the Sun of righteousness has shone upon us.... Today we escape from darkness, and through the light of the knowledge of God we are enlightened.... Today the Lord comes to be baptized so that mankind may be lifted up. Today the one who never has to bow bends his head before his servant.... Today we have acquired the kingdom of heaven that has no end.[1]

The psalms too praise the glory of God made visible in Christ at his baptism: "The waters have lifted up, O Lord, the waters have lifted up their thunder./Greater than the roar of mighty waters, more glorious than the surgings of the sea, the Lord is glorious on high" (Ps 93:3-4). "The waters saw you, O God, the waters saw you and trembled; the depths were moved with terror" (Ps 77:16). "Let the rivers clap their hands, and the hills ring out their joy at the presence

[1] *Byzantine Daily Worship*, pp. 599-600.

of the Lord: / For he comes, he comes to rule the earth" (Ps 98:8-9).

But Lord, Master, do all the waters lift up their voice and tremble? Do all the rivers clap their hands? Is not deep still "calling on deep in the roar of waters"? Are your people not still crying out, "Your torrents and all your waves swept over me" (Ps 42:7)? Have your poor ones stopped calling, "Save me, O God, for the waters have risen to my neck..../I have entered the waters of the deep and the waves overwhelm me./I am wearied with all my crying, my throat is parched./My eyes are wasted away from looking for my God" (Ps 69:1-3)? What of these waters, Lord – the endless streams of sorrow, the rivers of tears, the oceans of blood? Do they praise you, Lord? Those drowning in them, eyes wasted away from looking for your presence, are they too washed in the light of your joy?

I think of the drowning by day, and at night I dream of the waters that overwhelm them. "You withheld sleep from my eyes; I was troubled and could not speak./I thought of the days of long ago and remembered the years long past./At night I mused within my heart./I pondered and my spirit questioned" (Ps 77:4-6). My mind and my heart cannot fathom the depths of God – present yet absent, his love victorious yet thwarted every second, his Son's Kingdom come yet still coming. I turn away to read a light, charming novel, a kind of Christian fairytale. Suddenly a dying old plowman says, "Things be as they be," and suddenly a young girl feels "on the raw the burning touch of things as they are."[2] Lord, I think, where can I flee from your Spirit whom I can never find, or where can I see your face that I can never hide from?

As I write, it is mid-November. As you read, it could be anytime at all. I am on one side of the winter solstice; but wherever you are, let us look at the same bright darkness of the sun that the Church claimed for Christ: how light is reborn at the very moment it appears to die, how ice and snow are already pregnant with summer, how our baptized Master has drowned death and lives in glory at the heart of things just as they are.

I remember how as a child and long afterward I always thought of winter as a severe nuisance – not a tragedy, but certainly a painful inconvenience. In Cleveland it usually began mildly enough. November could be sleety and mean, but it could bring a long spell of cool clarity. Sometimes a low sun would shine day after day through the open trees, across the empty fields, and its light falling at just

---

[2]Elizabeth Goudge, *Gentian Hill* (New York: Coward-McCann, Inc., 1949), p. 258.

such a modest angle would reveal the secret of brown: a whole world deepening from palest buff of fallen leaves to beige of grasses across the shades of cornstalks, nearby paths, hills in the distance, still branches of oaks, and sparrows' wings down to the waiting earth almost the color of black bread. Especially there the brown world gleamed, quietly flashed back such sun as it got so that even under a gray November sky it showed a dimension of light not visible in the dazzle of snow, leaves, flowers, or July. Enclosed by brown, you sensed a different sort of passage from dark to light that could almost make you forget it was also taking you to winter.

But purely in time that passage seemed to narrow both before and behind you. At first you were carried by the last hurrahs of football, the feasting of Thanksgiving, and the certain hope of Christmas and its two-week holiday. Despite tests, snow flurries, and shopping, the slope of that passage usually felt too slight to arouse much fear, maybe even seemed to tilt upward those last few days (as slow-moving in their way as schooldays in June) before the vacation. Then, suddenly, you knew you were sliding downhill fast, encased in time. With a great rush Christmas blossomed and faded, the old year vanished, and the new one began. The Bowl games, for all their fancy names and hoopla, had a hollow ring. How could you forget that you had once again been dumped into January – an ice-hard tundra that stretched interminably away to April – when inside you breathed stale air all day long and outside the world hurt your face?

What did we do in those prehistoric days before we became old enough for cars and parties and dates, before television, before indoor rinks and pools or trips to ski-hills or midterm breaks in Florida, before covered malls and cross-country skiing? Not on the farm, of course; I mean in the city or the suburbs. We went to school. We read. We had basketball and movies and the radio. But what I most vividly remember doing during winter is delivering papers in it.

Is it any wonder winter became for me an image of bleakness? For most of my life it has stirred in me half-buried memories of trudging through cold grayness for several months each of the seven years that I was a suburban paperboy. On the worst days my eyelashes would freeze together as I pulled my papers on a sled, and I wore snowpants over my trousers or pajamas under them. Most of the time it wasn't bad, only unpleasant, the antithesis of fun: winter. The routine was dreary, but then it always was, even in spring when the days became suddenly so clear that my eyes would smart in the new light, or breezing through summer on my bike under the green canopy of maples and oaks and falling in love with the amazing shapes of clouds, or watching in the sweet autumn haze for the first star or the rising of the harvest moon. Winter only hurt my face a bit after all, made my feet cold and my clothes soggy, chilled my spirit with its darkness. Sodden mittens and a slightly frosted heart are a nuisance, not a disaster, light-years away, really, from a perpetually hungry body or a politically terrorized mind.

Still, if winter was not a season of anguish for me, its cold and dark, its physical hardness, etched on my flesh and brain a lesson I had already learned, to my shock, in my heart: that life was hard, that it was far more governed by necessity than it seemed to be, that it had a quality denser than rock, more relentless than tyrants. Delivering papers in winter taught me what my heart was trying to learn, what peasants and the victims of the horrors I was reading of every day and seeing each week in newsreels had to learn with far greater urgency—how to endure. But (as everyone already knows because no one who wants to live escapes the lesson of endurance) to endure is neither to melt into total passivity nor to freeze into a hardness steelier than that of the glacier pressing down on you. Albert Camus has written somewhere, "In the midst of winter I discovered within myself an invincible summer." Endurance is more than stoicism. It is the awareness, no matter how fragile, not just that spring will come, but that even now, more unyielding than the fact of death, there runs within a river of sunlight and glad songs. Winter insisted that I hope, and when all the waters of my world were frozen, I learned to believe in joy.

Epiphany? I must have heard the word because we burned our Christmas trees on "Twelfthnight," but I don't remember understanding what it meant until I read James Joyce in college. Theophany? I had one when I was seventeen, but I wouldn't have had it, or any of the others I have been given since, if God had not already showed me how to believe in joy. How did he do it? I know why he did it, but how could he have got through to me? Through my mother, my father, my brother, my grandparents, my friends, through Sunday school, my own genes, and my ancestors' faith—yes, certainly, and most of all through my own need, but now?

What do I mean, "how"? Isn't the answer simply "by the grace of the Holy Spirit"? But that is what I am trying to find out, to remember: when in those winters did I hear you, Father, or see you, Master, or feel your breath in me, Good One? I don't know, but when I look at that boy that I was, even when I recall the way he complained or dawdled or kicked at the last chunks of snow in March to hurry the coming of spring, I remember how he always knew the green of truly ordinary time and later found the secret of brown. I think of what else Elizabeth Goudge wrote about the old plowman: "It was only by the tranquillity with which he wore the burning garment of things as they are that he could reveal his innate knowledge that the hands that had put it upon him were the hands of love. And the old man said, 'And it be Christmas Eve, see.'"[3]

Yes, I do see, and I understand why I am writing now about Epiphany, the fullness of Christmas and the anticipation of Easter. And I understand why I insisted on entering the poustinia on the feast of Christ's baptism, even though the outer door had been removed for repair and I had to hang a blanket over the doorway to keep out some of the cold. I see, and then I know that what Karl Rahner said of Christmas describes Epiphany, a reality that the suburban paperboy I was came to know in the darkness and cold of winter: "It happens within you when you are quiet. It teaches you that you have learned to be alone. Trust that which is near: it is not empty."

What stillness did I have then, what knowledge of love, what peace in solitude, what trust? I do not know, but I know that I felt the fragility of my body, apparently the nearest thing to me, cracking from the hardness of winter invading all of me, and that I came to know how to endure—and to find my way to a river of joy within me that no cold could ever freeze. Then I did not see Jesus my Lord plunging himself into that river. I did not even see the blaze of "zero summer"—at midday when the sun turns snow to glory or at midnight when the stars become diamonds and sapphires underfoot. My epiphany was simply that the whole world, even winter, was a place where I could live and that my heart, even at its emptiest, could be a passage into beauty and freedom. I only began at 12 to learn what I am still beginning to learn, but I would not be beginning if I had not already begun.

Things as they are: later I would come to see the baptism of Christ as the Church sees it, as Annie Dillard, in *Holy the Firm*, sees it—as the revelation of God in the flesh taking upon himself the weight of all creation's moments, healing the broken, consecrating the beautiful, transfiguring all by his careful love into a new icon of his Father's glory. Later I would come to know, because Jesus my Master

---

[3]Ibid.

would teach me, how to see the grace of the Holy Spirit healing my own heart: I would watch him work in my brothers and sisters, and I would recognize that my eyes had been transfigured. Then, at 12, I saw very little, but I did see that a hard world, cold as winter, would yield to an inner gaze unafraid to look into the center of darkness and to hope.

THINGS AS THEY WILL BE

That's the way it is with things as they are: they do continue, and if you wanted to write about them forever, you'd forever have everything to write about—until Kingdom come. I am still pondering winter—the world's and mine—and I am still meditating on the Lord's plunge into the waters of all creation and on Elizabeth Goudge's plowman, who "wore the burning garment of things as they are" so tranquilly that he revealed "that the hands that had put it upon him were the hands of love." But the Kingdom will come, not the Kingdom of the Spirit—the Kingdom of faith, of sacrament, of Nazareth, of ordinary time, of the heart, of silence—but the Kingdom of Christ's full glory, where we will see the hands of love take from us the garment of things as they are and clothe us with the light of things as they will be.

I am still remembering my own discovery of the gateway of hope that led to the endless river of joy running within. The words of the old spiritual come to me, words that speak of the enormity of God's mercy and power and love, of God himself in Jesus: "So high you can't get over it, so low you can't get under it, so wide you can't go around it, you gotta go through that door!" Why sing, "gotta," even joyfully? If the hands that made the door are the hands of love, if the door itself is love, if in fact the door is Jesus, God himself in our flesh, why would anyone try to go over, under, or around it?

To put the question another way: why does the garment of things as they are burn? Why would we not want to be quiet or alone? Why mistrust what is near or fear that it might be empty? How did the fact of winter, its unavoidable hardness, become for me a physical experience of my heart's deep life? The questions are more than rhetoric or style. I'm asking them to reach toward the deeper question that lies beyond the obvious answers—family troubles, social upheaval, spiritual confusion, Satan, even rebellion against God. The answers are correct enough, as far as they go, but they don't go nearly far enough unless they push you toward that deeper question, make you hear the torrents and the raging waters and the groaning of all creation in the pangs of childbirth. Only when we are at sea with all the rest of the boat-people can we ask what we want to ask: "Who is this God who dares to identify himself with things as they are?" Then Jesus in the Jordan, endurance in the world's winter, the doorway of love into joy without end – in short, Epiphany and still shorter, the Gospel itself – *happen*: disclose the glorious freedom of the children of God, now and as we shall be.

"What is the answer, Gertrude?" Alice B. Toklas asked the dying Gertrude Stein, and from her bed Gertrude replied, "What is the question, Alice?" As if she didn't know. How can earth's waters shout both praise and agony so loudly? How can the earth's beauty break your heart with joy if God does not exist – and how can earth's pain break your heart with sorrow if he does? Who is this God who dares to weave this garment of fire?

I begin to see now what a treasure I was given during those winters when I delivered papers and began to learn that the world was both a home and a passage. Wholeness – that is what I began to learn: that the world is both beauty and pain, that joy lies hidden in both, especially where both meet. Until we know that things as they are burn terribly, more terribly than absolute zero or the center of the sun, we know nothing.

Do you see? The world will not get out of the way. We cannot freeze a sunrise any more than we can decree an end to tears. We can embrace the earth and kiss it, as Father Zossima urged. We can treasure it in our hearts and learn to love all its children. We can cultivate and shape it, harness its cruel volcanoes, soften its winters, and destroy forever this or that particular set of its wicked human systems. Marx and Nietzsche and Mao and all the revolutionaries are right: things as they are – the tyranny of disease, the torment of the poor, the alliance between power and death, the corruption of the little ones with lies and illusion – these are intolerable, an abomination of human agony, a mockery of the very idea of God. Yet look at the world their heirs have created. The world will not get out of the way. We can fondle it, analyze it, change it, ignore it, but it will not get out of the way. It will not yield to us except by our humble faith and hope in him who made and remade it.

Winter is the image of the final koan, the link that makes the green of ordinary time and the secret of brown come full circle, the cosmically right moment for the descent of Jesus into the waters — for God's embrace of everything that is.

> How long, O God, is the enemy to scoff?
> Is the foe to insult your name forever?
> Why, O Lord, do you hold back your hand?
> Why do you keep your right hand hidden?
>
> Yet God is our king from time past,
> The giver of help through all the land.
> It was you who divided the sea by your might,
> who shattered the heads of the monsters in the sea. . . .
> It was you who dried up ever-flowing rivers.
>
> Yours is the day and yours is the night,
> It was you who appointed the light and the sun:
> It was you who fixed the bounds of the earth:
> you who made both summer and winter.
>
> Remember this, Lord . . .
> let the poor and needy bless your name (Ps 74:10-13, 15-18, 20).

God, the one true God who made heaven and earth, has made summer and winter and all other contradictions, even those that contradict us, his special creation. He has "made the world firm, not to be moved" (Ps 93:1), so that in its very unyieldingness we might discover the doorway into joy: the submission that makes us both children of infinite love and masters of our own home and our own hearts begins as hope and ends as adoration.

All very well, perhaps, as a revelation of "winter" as God made it, but what of the winter we have made? What of my frozen heart as I plodded through the snow day after day, what of my godson's schizophrenia, my friend's cancer, my oldest friend's suicide, the sexual terrors that make my spiritual children weep, the ghosts and demons and sins that bind them so fast? What of Poland and Afghanistan, El Salvador and Nicaragua, Angola, Ethiopia, and Cambodia, what of the whole litany of nations whose names I speak into the Lord's mercy every day, each of them a crystal of light and a winter tundra of sorrow?

In the words of Annie Dillard, let me tell you how I see them all, baptized with Jesus, crucified and risen with him, wearing with him forever the garment of burning love that his Father's hands have woven:

> Christ is being baptized. The one who is Christ is there, and the one who is John. . . . The two men are bare to the waist. The one walks him

> into the water, and holds him under. His hand is on his neck. Christ is coiled and white under the water, standing on stones. He lifts from the water. Water beads on his shoulders. I see the water in balls as heavy as planets, a billion beads of water as weighty as worlds, and he lifts them up on his back as he rises. He stands wet in the water. Each one bead is transparent, and each has a world. . . . light and alive and apparent inside the drop: it is all there ever could be, moving at once, past and future, and all the people. I can look into any sphere and see people stream past me, and cool my eyes with colors and the sight of the world in spectacle perishing ever, and ever renewed. I do; I deepen into a drop and see all that time contains, all the faces and deeps of the worlds and all the earth's contents, every landscape and room, everything living or made or fashioned, all past and future stars, and especially faces, faces like the cells of everything, faces pouring past me talking, and going, and gone.[1]

If the revolutionaries have listened to the roar of the waters of grief and pain, and if they have seen those torrents and all the waves sweeping away the very throne of God himself, they have not seen what God did or heard the Word he has spoken – not over the chaos of the waters, but into that chaos. The Father claimed fatherhood not just for the winter or the night that he made; he claimed as his own as well the night our blindness fashioned, the winter our lovelessness formed from the heritage of love he gave us – and not just Adam and Eve. No matter how poor our parents may have been, what have you done with the love they gave you; what have I? Jesus became our present hope and our glory to come by going through the door of things as they are – of things as they have become because of us. With his own hands the Master wove the garment of things as they are into a mantle of love. He will not cease to help us wear it until its love soaks us through and through, so that "when he appears, we shall be like him, for we shall see him as he is" (1 Jn 3:2) – infinitely Beloved of the Father, everlastingly bright with the Spirit, all joy.

There are ways without end to say what Annie Dillard saw, what the Church will see until Christ clothes us with the flesh that will be like his, and he himself becomes our sun. This is one: the eternal Word of God became flesh, changeless Love immersed himself in the abyss of change, decay, rebellion, death, and God himself drowned death by drowning, rising, standing with us until his glory changes each most terrible thing that is into the way to joy without end. Or this, simply: when all the waters of your world are frozen,

---

[1] *Holy the Firm* (New York: Harper & Row, 1977), pp.69-71.

you will know a silent figure silently breaking the ice to stand in that coldness until all that is for you begins to become a sacrament of love. If you watch the Master being baptized, watch with your heart, you will see how bright they have all become – all the moments, all the sorrows, all the faces. Christ is in our midst. He is and he always will be. He is what will be.

"Walk through the winter," Jesus says. "Be still in the darkness, wash your brother's feet, love your enemy, embrace your death, and you will know that I am with you. That is my name – 'I will be there.' I am in everything that is, and behold, I make all things new."

Or with the finality of the canonical words themselves:

> Behold, the dwelling of God is with men. He will dwell with them, and they shall be his people, and God himself will be with them. He will wipe away every tear from their eyes, and death shall be no more, neither shall there be mourning nor crying nor pain any more, for the former things have passed away. And he who sat upon the throne said, "Behold, I make all things new" (Rev 21:3-5).

MEETING

You
You made me wait
You and I and this blank page
We are listening to my birthday rain
We are watching all the trees
Burst into October light.
How can we be waiting together
When I am waiting for you?
How can your impossible silence
Touch my face like a kiss?
How can my body end so precisely
At boot-soles, folds of clothes,
Curves of skin, ends of hair,
At the limit of my sight
On the misted, golden ridge
Where I am still looking for you,
When all of me is running out
Like photons spilling from a nova
And I am filling all that isn't you
With me
With my waiting,
So that when you touch
The least somewhere of time
You must touch me
Who am now the full horizon of emptiness?

And how could I
Be facing you there –
Dark to dark, nothing –
In the farthest shallows of everywhere
As all of tidy space

Sends its last bits foaming past me
Still so visibly, tangibly far
From your unmoving feet
Into the reaches of nowhere?
How could I when
Back here in October
You are waiting,
You and this now marked page,
With all the words I've ever written
And all the ones you've never said
Like bright forests of birthday leaves
For us to stroll in
Together?
We are watching all the world
Bloom into final light
And I wonder, Jesus,
Does it matter how or where at last
I touch you with my eyes
When I could be anywhere at all
With so confidently waiting
You here?